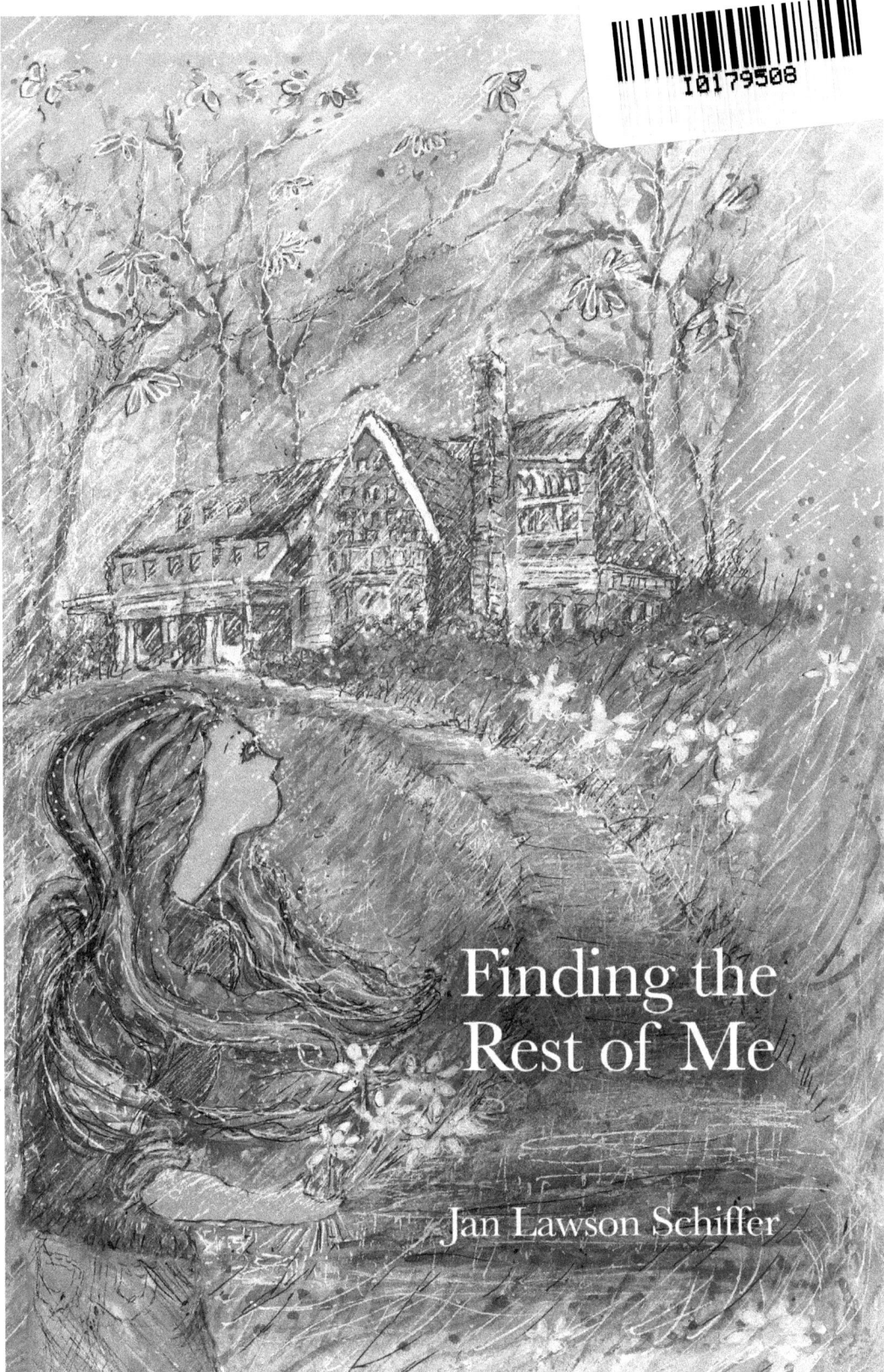

FINDING THE REST OF ME

JAN LAWSON SCHIFFER

FINDING THE REST OF ME ©2024 JAN SCHIFFER

All Rights Reserved.
Reproduction in whole or in part without the authors' permission is strictly forbidden. All photos and/or copyrighted material appearing in this publication remains the work of its owners.

Cover illustration by Lynda C. Porter
Author photo by Hilly Schiffer Dobner
Edited by Lynn Lauber & Mary Popham
Book designed by Fishtail Publishing

Published in the USA by Fishtail Publishing
Columbus, Ohio

Paperback: 979-8-9919002-0-1

DEDICATION

To my children and grandchildren, for whom this journey began.
Each one of you is a treasured blessing to me.

CONTENTS

Preface..ix

Part I: The Journey

1. The Word...3
2. The Nudge...7
3. The Search..14
4. The Call...23
5. First Love..36
6. Birth Mom..44
7. Adoptive Parents..49
8. The Trifold...55
9. A Day In The Home - 33 Stairs......................................65

Part II: Other Family Members

10. Barb's Dad and Mine..73

11. The Connection Nudge...77

12. Barb's Girls..81

13. My Grandparents..85

14. She Lingers..94

15. Transitions...101

Part III: The Side Trip Along The Way

16. Home - A Providential, Protected Property..............109

17. The Introduction to My First Home........................115

18. Tours And Correspondences....................................122

19. Finding The Rest Of Me: Investigating My First Home...............139

20. Puzzle Pieces..149

References..154

Acknowledgments..156

—PREFACE—

I have witnessed many forms of adoption throughout my lifetime. Three immediate family members are adoptees, as well as close friends. Many in my life have adopted children. Some adoptees decided to have a relationship with members of their biological families. There are those who have enjoyed wonderful reunions, while others have experienced heartbreak. Many have no desire to know their biological family. A precious few didn't know of their adoption, and that secret was meant to last a lifetime. As unique individuals with equally unique life experiences, we possess our own set of beliefs and life goals. Each will decide how their own story plays out.

This is my journey with the help of a few nudges along the way.

"It doesn't matter anyway, because you were adopted," my cousin Winni yelled at me. These words echoed in the recesses of my mind for over 32 years. I learned their meaning when I was six years old, but didn't allow that knowledge to translate into action until I was thirty-eight.

At sixty-nine, I've just completed the 30th anniversary of my journey's commencement. It has been quite the adventure. I expected falls, setbacks, roadblocks, detours, as well as bumps and bruises along the way. What I didn't foresee were the "off-road" friends I would make or the curves that would lead me to new destinations not highlighted on my original map. I believe that just like any great trip, there are beautiful side trips if we willingly make the time for them.

This book illuminates my path to my biological family. My journey has taken me to the unwed mother's home of my birth and taught me about the woman who had the vision to believe this home was necessary in 1905.

Proceeding down that specific path to my first home, an unwed mother's home, has afforded me the privilege of entering the lives of two amazing women connected to the Home; the proprietor at the time, and a woman who shared a mutual interest in the Home due to her experience as a resident fourteen years after my birth mother inhabited it.

It has all unfolded like an incredible trip to a new place never encountered before. I took in the sights that were in the brochure. Then, voila, something novel and exciting captured my interest. Each side trip became some of the best parts of the adventure, and I'm left with a deep sense of gratitude for having taken each one. As I have discovered, it's been a journey worth taking!

Part I:
The Journey

—Chapter 1—
The Word

My younger cousin Winni was five, and I was six, innocent youngsters in most ways. As children of Greatest Generation parents, we grew up in families that sheltered us by keeping secrets considered too complicated for us to understand.

Our parents and grandparents had much to process while living through the Great Depression and two world wars! Making ends meet to provide for a family was as much, if not more of a challenge than it is today. War disrupts families and many family members never come home. Nothing was easy during those times, and only adult ears were supposed to hear serious conversations regarding the choices made.

The comment "children should be seen and not heard," was mentioned more than once in my home in Lima, Ohio. My parents, 35 years older than I was, strictly adhered to the philosophy that children should not argue or pry into the affairs of adults. But one secret eventually surfaced.

The year was 1960, and my cousin Winni had arrived for her annual summer visit. My grandparents met us halfway in the small, pleasant town of Byhalia, Ohio. At a set time, we would converge on the shoulder of the road near a small country school. After a short conversation and sometimes a picnic lunch, Winni and her suitcase headed home with us, and Grandpa and Grandma Lawson drove back to their home in Columbus, Ohio.

At the end of the week, pleasantries and an abbreviated recap of the week's activities were shared. Later in the summer, my folks would escort me to my grandparents' home, where another cousin week would begin.

And so it was that my cousin and I were enjoying a warm summer weekend afternoon, riding our tricycles on the tree-lined cement sidewalk in front of our modest Cape Cod home in Lima, Ohio. It was a peaceful, quiet neighborhood composed of young families with several children or older couples who had lived there since the late 1940s.

We rode back and forth, back and forth, laughing, racing, and giggling as the wind blew through our hair. Mine was a short pixie cut, perfect for my straight brown, cowlicked hair, which stood straight up when the breeze caught it. The word cowlick describes the way a cow licks her calves, creating a swirling pattern on their hair. Mom never licked my hair, but she did lick her hand to pat down the uncooperative, fly-away hairs. Winni had curly, shoulder-length brown hair. Years later, as teenagers, we would laugh about how jealous we had always been of each other's hair.

Occasionally, we traded tricycles. Mine was a plain blue one, redeemed by a metal bugle horn with a black rubber ball attached. The horn made a loud goose call sound when squeezed. However, Winni had an amazing Pluto face on the front of her trike, which definitely made it the cool and favored trike.

The day was perfect for riding up and down the sidewalk. All was sweetness and light until Winni decided it was time to switch trikes again. I was riding on the cool tricycle and wasn't ready to switch yet. Although younger, my cousin was typically the one who dictated our play. It might have been because she was an only child and accustomed to having her way.

In fairness to her, I was almost an only child, considering my brother was ten years older. Perhaps my placement in our family caused me to have more of a peacekeeper personality. Whatever the reason, conflict of any kind upsets me, and I went to great lengths to resolve it when it occurred. However, this time was different. I didn't think I had been on her trike long enough, so I requested a few more minutes. She was riding in front of me and adamantly refused my request.

We argued back and forth until she hopped off my trike, stomped toward me, and began pulling her bike's handlebar, rocking me. Her face was fuming, and I knew she was irate. The motion made me mad, and I finally shouted, "Stop!"

She flashed a mean smile in my direction, pushed the bike away from her, and said, "Well, it doesn't matter anyway, because you were adopted!"

Adopted? I'd never heard that word before, let alone understood its meaning. But the word obviously meant something negative, given her attitude. So, of course, I responded with an abrupt, "No, I wasn't!" even though I didn't know what I was defending.

A series of *yes, you were* and *no, I wasn't,* grew in intensity and volume. I couldn't understand why she had called me this. Was it possible that she knew a secret about me? Tears welled up in my eyes, and eventually streamed down my face. I couldn't bear to look at her. I got off of her trike and ran up the cement steps to my house.

I planned to throw open the door and call out for my dad, who, in my world, could answer every question and fix any problem. Surely, he would be on my side and tell Winni to stop calling me that word. He had been enjoying an afternoon nap in his easy chair, but the outdoor commotion awakened him. By the time I reached the porch he was standing inside the screen door with a stern look on his face. He calmly opened the door for me.

Without a word, I followed him inside to his chair, where he sat down. He tapped his left leg with his hand, inviting me to crawl into his lap. I told him what Winni had called me. After I did, he began to speak calmly and softly, and I wish I could remember all the words he used to comfort me. What I do remember is that he told me he and Mom loved me and that adoption meant that I was chosen. He repeated the word chosen several times as he lovingly told me how special I was to our family. It never entered my mind to ask if my brother was chosen.

That day on his lap I decided "adopted" was not an awful word. An adopted child is chosen and special. After accepting Dad's explanation,

I was certain he would address Winni's unacceptable outburst. Instead, he didn't appear to be upset with anyone, so I held onto my anger.

When I slid off of his lap, I saw Winni leaning against the doorway quietly crying. Although I was still upset with her, her face made me sad. My dad called her over to him, spoke to her for a moment, gathered us together for a group hug, and told us to go back outdoors and play.

That was it. My dad always had a way of putting people at ease with his soft-spoken presence, one of the many qualities that made him, in many of his clients' estimation, a gentleman's attorney. He could de-escalate a situation with his calm demeanor and well-chosen words. I was calm but remained confused and unsettled.

And how did Winni feel? Was she scared of the repercussions she might endure because of her outburst? Dad opened the door and sent us outside to figure it out, but neither of us had the maturity to work through this obstacle. No one referenced "the word," and somehow, we kept our closeness for the remaining days before she went back home.

I wondered what that trip home felt like for my cousin. I wondered if she had to account for her actions or if, like me, life returned to normal.

However, that year, I didn't stay with my grandparents, and I thought I knew why. This adoption thing was unsettling, and it pricked each person involved. The irony is that my cousin was born out of wedlock and lived with her mother. I didn't consider it odd, and my parents didn't believe I needed to know why her dad was not present, especially because I never asked. If I didn't ask, there was no reason to discuss it.

Several years ago, in a writing class, I found out exactly how my cousin came to know about my adoption. I reached out to her, and there was a simple explanation. She had overheard her mother and our aunt talking about their brother- and sister-in-law's decision to keep my adoption a secret from me. They disagreed with my parents and thought I had a right to know.

I didn't believe Winni when she said she thought she was doing me a favor by telling me about my adoption; that she thought I should know. If the circumstances had been different, I might have agreed. However, I thought it was simply her way of hurting me because she was not getting her way in our tug-of-war with the trike. We were children with child-like responses to upsetting situations.

To my knowledge, only our family and their closest friends at the time of my birth knew about my adoption. Winni and I had no idea how that exchange would affect our rather tumultuous relationship over the years. Our family was small, and we were together often. I thought her comment on that lovely summer afternoon was her way of saying, "I know something you don't know and I am using it to hurt you." Only recently have I dug deeper into the underlying hurt I felt that day. I discovered there is a blessing in it. Had she not spoken "the word," I might never have pursued its meaning when I was older, and my life would look very different today. Instead, I became one of those who knew I was adopted.

—Chapter 2—
The Nudge

I'd never felt a strong urge to locate my birth mother or birth father. However, after I married and gave birth to three children, I wondered if it would be beneficial for them to know their biological health history and what they might encounter in the future.

I would look at their features and wonder who they looked like. But I didn't want to take the chance of potentially hurting my adoptive parents' feelings by searching for those answers. After all, they had kept my adoption a secret from most people for years. Would I open a wound that would seep forever after my discovery? Would their love remain strong if I breached the confidentiality that was established over the years? I always let those thoughts, temptations from my perspective, settle back into the crevices of my subconscious rather than confront the mom and dad who loved and took such good care of me. Those thoughts were usually fleeting.

But not this time. In 1992, two years after my father-in-law passed, my world changed, and my outlook shifted. My perspective and priorities altered. My heart remolded.

It began gradually, after watching a Phil Donahue program about adoption with the Concerned United Birthparents' founder, Lee Campbell, as his guest. Campbell talked about her pregnancy at 16 years of age and why she gave her son up for adoption. She described her decision to ask the adoptive parent for permission to meet him sixteen years later. I don't recall ever being introduced to an individual who spoke so freely about an issue so close to my heart. She was passionate about the choices, demonstrated sincere compassion while answering the audience's pointed questions and judgemental comments. Her reasoning intrigued me and she impressed me with her composure. Her demeanor captivated me, and I clung to her every word.

I will never forget Lee Campbell's story and the mental picture she drew of the perception of the unwed mother in the 1960s. I suppose the show was a rebroadcast because she was on four other times from 1979 to 1984. That show's message would swirl around in my mind for days. I was thirty-eight years old and happily married with three wonderful, healthy children: Nate (16), Brian (13), and Hillary (7). My husband, George, worked shifts at our local refinery, I had a full-time job as a paraprofessional in an elementary classroom with severely behaviorally handicapped children, and we were busy with all our children's various activities. I didn't need a diversion; I had no time for it. However, I felt a sense of urgency that I could not dismiss.

I only shared my unsettled spirit with my husband. Then, I started having trouble sleeping at night. I thought about the program during the day and had nightmares about it at night. Every time I would pray, I *heard* nothing, but clearly felt this nudge to contact my birth mother to say, "Thank you."

But why? That was the nagging question during my restless nights and my distraction during those disturbing days. I was fighting the urge to act on what I thought was an unrealistic and futile illusion. In my mind, I shouldn't pursue a thought that I perceived to be a deception. It was only my mind wandering into the world of "what if." What if my imagination was running amuck after hearing all the adoption talk? It would lead nowhere beneficial.

Not long after the Donahoe program aired, I was called to my pastor's office. He recalled an editorial I wrote in 1990 for our local newspaper that focused on the upcoming "Rally for Life" the following day in Washington, DC. This is how it read:

Lima News - April 27, 1990
Give your child a chance; consider adoption option

Editor:

The debate rages on. Keep the baby! Abort the fetus.

As we approach the "Rally for Life 90" to be held in Washington D.C. tomorrow, I am compelled to appeal to the pregnant girl or woman. You have been informed or counseled about your choices, maybe. But have you considered the case for adoption?

Over 30 years ago, the process of adoption was much different. The birth mother often knew nothing about the adoptive parents, had little or no control over that process, and upon completion of record keeping, the matter was closed.

No longer is that the case. There are doors open to you in the selection process itself. Good, loving and nurturing adoptive parents exist, too.

Perhaps you are unable or unwilling to provide for this new life. There are others who desire that privilege.

For those of us rearing more than one child, we are acutely aware of the fact that no two children are alike. There will never be another person just like the one within your womb today. That person is unique.

Are there successful adoptions taking place today? Yes, I consider myself to be one of them. I am grateful that my birth mother sacrificed nine months of her life for me. I am thankful that I was placed into the arms of a loving, nurturing adoptive family. After over 30 years, I continue to be proud of my "roots" (biological and adoptive).

My situation is not unique. I know families who have raised adoptive children no differently than they would have their biological children. More importantly, I know of families who still desperately wait years for that opportunity.

Still undecided? Check out the adoption option. Call the agencies in our area dealing with adoptions. Give your child a chance. Give him/her nine months. The life you save is irreplaceable.

J. Schiffer, Lima

My pastor referenced this editorial when we met in his office that afternoon. He told me about a congregant who was feeling devastated because both her adoptive and biological mothers recently died. He didn't know any details of my adoption story, but said I kept coming to his mind as he prayed for wisdom in consoling her. I questioned whether I could offer her solace during this catastrophic chapter in her life. I felt helpless, because I had no idea what it meant to have both moms in my life. But I understood she was heartbroken, and I agreed with my pastor to reach out to her.

Our conversation was limited, and her grief was overwhelming. The next few nights, I dreamed about her sad story and also about Lee Campbell's desire to reunite with her son. I woke up the next morning, prayed for wisdom, and searched the scriptures for peace. It seemed my only answer was in the form of a "nudge" from God.

Later that same month, I watched a program on our local Christian TV station involving the lady who stood behind the counter at our local credit union, where we did business. Janine shared her story of a reunion with her biological mother. It sounded lovely, but I turned it off almost immediately. I was conflicted. I loved my life and my family. It would be complicated. How could I tell my adoptive parents that God had advised me to find my biological mother in order to thank her? Why now, they might ask? I was Walt and Maxine Lawson's daughter. No one in my parents' generation, or outside my immediate family, had ever mentioned my adoption in my presence, so I assumed they didn't pass the information to the next generation. It felt like I would dredge up the past with no certainty of a pleasant outcome. I was not comfortable negotiating through the unknown, particularly since I was the one instigating the action.

My turmoil escalated. Getting less sleep and becoming more anxious was my new state of existence. Within this same time period, I read a *Guidepost* devotion about our adoption into God's family and heard a Focus on the Family radio program, featuring a psychologist from the Minirth Meier Clinic as their guest. The topic was adoption. I was never so inundated with information regarding adoption.

In late February 1992, Janine walked into the Credit Union and stood behind me with her three young children. Her youngsters reminded me of mine: two older boys (one with brown hair and one with light blonde hair) and a daughter. They were a younger version of my family. Someone in line mentioned the TV program where she shared her adoption experience, and Janine began telling stories of how wonderful it was to feel "complete." She must have noticed the confused look on my face because she asked what I was thinking. At that moment, I did not know why I opened up to her. I began asking her questions, and before we departed, we had each other's phone numbers. Several hours-long calls ensued, and I felt undeniable relief. Someone who had recently chosen to take this journey as an adoptee was providing me a safe, comforting outlet to express my deepest concerns. Her advice was to move forward and act on my "nudge," and I told her I would continue to think about it.

The first two months of 1992 were tumultuous. *Tell her thank you. She deserves to know you are alive and well.* These phrases reverberated in the depths of my being with unrelenting perseverance. I had trouble going to sleep and staying asleep, and, when I awoke, my first cognitive thought was, Tell her thank you, today.

One morning, before I could hear the words ringing out again, I surrendered to them with, "OK, Lord. Your will, not mine, but You will have to guide me through it." This was the moment my journey began in earnest. I requested my original birth certificate from the Ohio Health Department. Who could that hurt? It was just information; there seemed to be no harm in it. No contact needed to result from it.

Nudges. The more I've researched, the more I've learned that they can come from many sources. Our subconscious may present a situation we haven't completely resolved. Others would say it's the devil acting as an angel. I have a friend who would argue that mine was not a God nudge but the universe telling me that this act of expressing gratitude to the source of my existence would be in the realm of positive karma. As my journey unfolded, I did not doubt the source, and this gave me peace.

—Chapter 3—

The Search

The process of locating my biological mother was relatively simple in 1992. In every adoption, there is an original, and an amended birth certificate. The original birth certificate, including the name of the child and the names of the birth parents, remains sealed along with any other adoption records. The amended birth certificate is the only one handed to the adoptive parents after the adoption is final, and it contains their names and their child's adopted name. In my case, my adoptive parents received the certificate on October 13, 1954, eight months after I became their foster child.

This was the era of closed adoptions. Sealing those records and omitting the birth parents' names in documents was an attempt to protect the birth mother and father's privacy in closed adoptions. This was a common practice in the Baby Scoop Era.

Adoptions were on the rise after WWII. Sexual behavior was more liberal, and birth control availability was limited. There were significantly more premarital pregnancies, which was thought to account for a rise in newborn adoptions. Some thought unwed mothers may have psychological defects and were told their newborns would be better off if given up for adoption.

If a pregnant woman was feeling shunned, and if her family was financially able, she left home and went away to one of the many unwed mother maternity homes. Family members and friends were often told that the oftentimes young girl was visiting a relative who needed her help. The staff in the unwed mother's home rarely encouraged the mother to keep her baby. Instead, most institutions recommended adoption to the mother as her only option. Their emphasis was to give the unwed mother the life skills she needed after her delivery, but without an infant.

In the late 60s and early 70s, the Women's Movement changed the way women thought about themselves and encouraged them to take control of their own bodies. Women developed a new identity when birth control pills were legalized and family planning was available, due to federal funding. The legalization of abortion significantly contributed to a new sense of freedom for females.

Roe vs. Wade changed not only the course of the adoption explosion but also the identity and description of 70s women, their bodies, and their right to choose. I read the book *Our Bodies, Ourselves: A Book by and for Women* from cover to cover in 1974 when I was the Teen Director at the Lima YWCA. I thought it provided valuable health information and tips, as well as revolutionary ideas for women and girls. I wanted to *be* informed just as much as I wanted to inform the teenage girls with whom I was working.

I requested the Affidavit of Adopted Person form, filled it out, and had it notarized in March 1992. I had to enclose at least two forms of identification and a check for $5.00. I sent the documentation to the Ohio Department of Health with a request for my original birth certificate. Since I had a closed adoption, my age was no longer a factor. In 1992, an adoptee in Ohio needed to be eighteen years of age in order to receive a copy of one's original certificate of birth and copies of other papers that were included in the adoption envelope.

For me, the most challenging aspect of sending the documentation was finding someone to notarize the document because I rarely talked openly about my adoption. Fortunately, I found a trusted friend who notarized it for me. I mailed the required form, and I received my official birth certificate and my certificate of adoption decree from the Probate Court on April 13, 1992.

I was eager to discover my biological mother's actual name, and there it was on the first line: Barbara Ann Copeland. My first thought was the song "Barbara Ann," written by Fred Fassert in 1958, and made famous by the Beach Boys in 1965. I began humming the catchy tune as I wondered how she might have felt about having a song with her name as its title.

My eyes quickly focused on all the details and facts regarding my birth date, time of birth, county of birth, registrar's number, and doctor's signature. They were the same on both documents. I knew the line for the parents' names and my birth name would be different. They were specific to the original and amended birth certificates.

The name on the original birth certificate surprised me. I was named Bernice Anne. How curious. I had not considered the name given to me at birth. Were there other family members, perhaps a great-grandmother, with that name? Bernice seemed like an older person's name.

What I realized that day was that my birth mother, Barbara, was all alone at the time of my birth. There was no father listed. Also, I learned I wasn't born in a hospital. As a teenager, I'd been told that my place of birth was St. Ann's Hospital, which opened in 1908 and was called St. Ann's Infant Asylum and Home for Unwed Mothers. I considered the name Infant Asylum a strange one. The word asylum seemed to befit an orphan or a refugee requiring protection after leaving their native country. Or, in this case, the mother's womb.

My original birth certificate stated I was born in the Friends Rescue Home, located at 245 N. Powell Ave., in Columbus, Ohio. On my amended birth certificate, that box was left blank. I wasn't familiar with that street, but began to wonder if my Grandpa Lawson, who drove a Columbus city bus, might have known it, but sadly, he was no longer alive to ask.

I found another surprise on the line stating the city or village where my biological mother was a resident. It was Lima, Ohio, which had been my hometown since my adoption. Since I was born in Columbus, Ohio, I had assumed that my birth mother lived in Columbus.

My birth mom's street address was also unfamiliar to me, but within the Lima city limits. I opened our current city phone book, but there was no Barbara Copeland listed on 1004 N. Jefferson. However, there was a Berniece, with a different spelling, Copeland on Devonshire Dr. That address was in my subdivision, and I had driven by the house frequently. My amended birth certificate also spelled my name differently—Bernice Ann—rather than Bernice Anne, the name on my original birth certificate. Did I have an aunt living right around the corner from me?

I would have to wait and check that out another day. It was late, but I returned to the birth certificate for a few more minutes. The rest of the information was consistent with my amended birth certificate. I was thrilled to be holding the original in my hands. It was a beginning, and I felt an unexpected sense of excitement at the prospect of discovering more information.

I didn't begin the research to locate my biological mother's whereabouts right away. I received the documentation on a Wednesday. I had very little time to absorb its contents, because the following day I drove to Columbus to visit my Aunt Tanny, Winni's mom. This trip had been planned for weeks, and I didn't want to miss it. We were rarely together, and thoroughly enjoyed spending an afternoon catching up on each other's lives. I said nothing about my recent discoveries. The day before had been an introduction to a new universe, where I was just becoming familiar with my birth world. It would take a while to process the information, and I certainly was not in a mental state to share it with anyone. It was good to have time on the road to think through all of my options moving forward.

The next day was Good Friday, and my dad was having an outpatient procedure. I sat with my mom in the waiting room most of the day. It was a long day, and we were all exhausted. They were informed that more procedures were in his future, but Dad was optimistic that all would go well.

On Saturday, I prepared for our Easter dinner and shuffled my sons to baseball practices, while my husband worked. After church on Sunday, our family enjoyed a traditional Easter meal together with Mom and Dad. Everything appeared "normal," but inside, my heart felt otherwise.

Six days after first seeing my original birth certificate, I began the research to locate my biological mother. It seemed like so much longer because so much had transpired in those six days.

For a few days, I considered different scenarios regarding the information I would find. It hadn't even occurred to me that my birth mother wasn't alive. God would not have led me on this journey if she weren't, would He?

My journal entry said that on Tuesday, April 21st, 1992, my feet couldn't fly quickly enough to the local library and courthouse to uncover my biological past. The kids and I were on Spring break, and as luck would have it, my husband worked afternoons that week. That allowed me a few morning hours before I needed to be home for the kids. I was looking forward to the challenge; the places where my research would take me were already familiar territory.

I had developed valuable skills by working in our county law library, across the street from my dad's law practice. Typically, an attorney's child received the summer job of assisting the law librarian, and he had secured it for me. In high school, I had begun working the week after school ended, in the summer after my senior year. The law library, housed in the Allen County Courthouse, was a fascinating place to work. Built in 1884, it possessed a lovely sandstone façade. In 1974, two years after I graduated from Lima Senior High school, the courthouse was in the National Register Of Historic Places. It was easy to see why; it was a magnificent structure, inside and out. I enjoyed climbing the beautifully appointed, wide marble stairs leading up to the fourth floor, where the library was located.

It was certainly an interesting and unique environment, and I loved to watch the law librarian, her pure white hair in an immaculate bun, attentively consider the request of each attorney as she secured just the right book, document, or folder in warp speed. She was incredible, and I often wondered where she would go after hearing the lawyer's request.

I might have recognized only half the words spoken, but that didn't deter me. My dad thought it funny when I asked him if he had something like an attorney's Thesaurus that I could take to work with me. My job was filing all the updated court decisions and revisions as they came into the library, which was daily. I asked the librarian if the lawyers had to pay for this service. She told me it cost the lawyers $5.00 a year when the law library first opened. Many became lifetime members, at a cost of $75.00, in the early 1900s. It was there that I learned how to find legal documents in the courthouse, as well. Often, I delivered an errant document to its proper location. On those occasions, I would overhear conversations regarding many legal matters. It groomed me for the task at hand, locating my birth mother. Of course, Google and Ancestry.com were not yet available, so it would have to be a paper trail.

I had the address where my birth mother had lived thirty-eight years prior to my investigation. So, I went to the public library to uncover information in the city directories about people living in the county. Immediately, I checked out my first lead, Berniece Copeland, who I thought might be an aunt. I discovered she had lived much of her life in a town nearby, but the family and the years didn't match mine. Dead end.

Next, I discovered a woman named Barbara Copeland who was living at 1004 N. Jefferson with her sister, Shirley, the year I was born! That was the same address that was on my original birth certificate. Next door to them lived John and Sylvia Grouver, who I soon learned was my maternal grandmother.

I continued to add more family members to my list and verified each name by age and their location in proximity to the Jefferson Avenue address. There was no Barbara Copeland in the city directory for several years after 1954. Dead end, or so I thought.

I drove back down to the courthouse to follow leads on other Copelands I'd found: Shirley, Sylvia, and Lawrence. Another Lawrence Copeland turned out to be my maternal grandfather. It was there that I discovered a marriage license dated May 1955. The couple was Barbara Ann Copeland and Bernard Crawford Hasson. Perhaps my life puzzle was coming together.

I thought of the name given to me by my birth mother: Bernice Anne Copeland. Bernice, maybe for Bernard and Anne, a variation of Barbara's middle name. As I made a copy of the document, I felt someone watching me from another room. When I looked up, a familiar set of eyes met mine. It was the probate judge, who was a good friend of my parents and a very kind man to me. He had a welcoming smile and always made me feel comfortable when in his presence at events in the past. I knew he was an adoptee, too.

He invited me into his office and, within minutes, I was sitting across the desk from him, sharing my discoveries and asking for his advice. He listened intently and took the time to tell me a bit of his own adoption story before suggesting two options. His advice was that I either find all the information by myself, which could take a long time and may not give me the correct information, or allow children's services to document the facts, contact Barbara for me, and ask her for a meeting. I believed my best option was to do it myself and not involve anyone else. I wanted to thank her in my way, and thought the agency would only ask if she wanted to contact me. I told him I really appreciated his advice and left feeling very grateful for his counsel. We never spoke of it again. That completed day one's research.

Day two found me back at the courthouse as soon as they opened that morning. It was then that I discovered Bernard, my presumed biological father's 1990 death notice and will. I learned I could have a full-blooded sister who received nothing, according to his will. My eyes filled with tears. It was the apparent rejection, not his passing, that produced my tears. I didn't even know her, but the words on the page saddened me. I continued to look through the information and finally came upon their divorce document. My half, or full sister was born in 1955, a year before their divorce, in 1956.

The next step was to locate another marriage license, death certificate, or any other document pertaining to Barbara Copeland Hasson. Perseverance paid off. I uncovered a marriage license for Barbara Copeland Hasson and Kenneth Morris in 1971. I couldn't wait to follow that lead to the library and back to the city directories. Instead, I slipped into the city planner's office, in the courthouse, and borrowed their directory. There it was. Kenneth and Barbara Morris were living at 1016 Woodland Drive. How exciting! My fingers felt numb as I closed the book. My birth mother lived in Lima, Ohio.

After climbing into my van, it took forever for me to buckle my seatbelt because my hands were trembling. Should I drive over there to her house now? Yes. I just couldn't wait. I'd only drive by. All the way over, I thought about the letter I would write to this special woman who I always had believed lived miles away from me. Instead, she practically lived in my backyard; less than eight miles separated us from one another. All these years living in the same town, I didn't know there were blood relatives living so close to me. I was overwhelmed.

I said a brief prayer as I reached the corner of Woodland Avenue and turned onto her street. I was nervous as a cat, and I didn't want to do anything to arouse suspicion as I slowly drove by the white brick ranch home.

I turned around in a driveway up the street and drove back by, from the other direction this time. I saw a large German Shepherd and what appeared to be a doghouse in the backyard that I had not noticed before. I had to smile since this wasn't surprising to me. I am also very fond of dogs.

When I passed by the front of the house that next time, I noticed a woman peering out the glass window of the French double-door entry who had not been there the first time. Was she my biological mother? Would this be my initial glimpse of her since learning of her existence? From my street view, she appeared shorter than I had imagined, and her bouffant style hair was light colored, not dark like mine. My heart skipped a beat at the sight of her, and I thought it might never return to its proper rhythm.

My knees shook, and I couldn't get away from there quickly enough. During my seventeen-minute drive home, my head spun and my heart pounded. I didn't realize I would be so overcome with emotion. I had not expected this process to come together so quickly or easily. As I headed home, the one thought that couldn't escape me was wondering if she could have been thinking about me at that moment, or if I ever crossed her mind.

I had done my due diligence and knew that I had found her, or at least her house. Now, it was the details that I wondered about whenever I wasn't working or caring for my family. I had no trouble sleeping now. However, I woke up early, and questions immediately filled my mind. *Should I reveal this information to my mom and dad? If so, when? Should I really contact my birth mother? If so, how? Should I leave a paper trail? What if her current husband and my half, or full sister didn't know I existed? How would I know when it was the right time?*

There were times I had to remind myself why I was even contemplating this course of action. Eight days earlier, I had been holding the original birth certificate and a final decree of adoption document in my hands for the first time.

It seemed more complicated now that living, breathing people were involved in this nudge. Still, the exciting part was that my birth mother was alive, and an opportunity to thank her might one day present itself.

—Chapter 4—

The Call

Several evenings later, I walked into my parents' house with the news I had been reluctant to share. I was not afraid, but I was definitely uncertain as to my exact words and how they would be received. I believed God led me to this decision, so fear was not a factor. My husband offered to come with me for moral support, but I knew this was a discussion reserved for three. It was a Sunday night, and it was unlike me to invite myself over to visit since the kids and I would be getting prepared for school on Monday morning.

Dad greeted me at the door with a hug, while Mom was comfortably sitting in her favorite upholstered chair with a book in her lap, peering over her shoulder and above her glasses at me. I flashed her a quick smile and greeting. Dad led me into the living room, where I sat on my usual couch cushion across from Mom. Slowly, she bookmarked the last page she had been reading, closed the book, and slipped it onto the ottoman in front of her. All the while, she was deliberately studying me, trying to decipher my emotional state.

In the meantime, Dad walked over to his easy chair, sat down, propped up his legs on his ottoman, and immediately inquired about the family. Any conversation involving my Dad always began with him politely inquiring about the other person's family. He would listen for hours if someone was so inclined to "bend his ear." It seemed like his thoughtful questions continued forever. I waited patiently. I didn't want an abrupt or uncomfortable segue into the story that had led me to them that night.

It was remarkably easy to begin. I never seem to give God enough credit when I pray for something, like the words He wants me to speak. There are moments when I think God might need to take a minute to consider my request and get back to me later instead of believing He is the all-knowing, omniscient One who knows me and my needs before I even pray. Tonight, I was counting entirely on Him. This conversation had the potential of being the most difficult one I would have with my parents, and I prayed that the One who nudged me would speak through me.

I gave my parents the whole story and the complete background. The barrage of overwhelming incoming data regarding adoption, the God nudges and inability to sleep, the decision to send for the documents and the peace I felt after doing so, the details regarding the search, and my current intentions. There was a bit of laughter when I told them about talking with the probate judge, and my familiarity with the courthouse. Then, there was a thought-provoking pause before Dad spoke. I was familiar with the silence he required while gathering his thoughts before speaking.

He was very curious about my investigative process, while Mom simply listened. I had already decided that I would leave out what I learned about the man who might be my biological father and my half, or full sister. After all, this was about thanking my biological mother. Mr. Hasson, my biological father, had died two years earlier, and I wasn't planning to contact my sister, so no other information seemed necessary. After allowing them a few minutes to process it all, I told them I would not think of contacting her behind their backs. Their opinion had always been important to me. Their judgment was less of a concern as I felt I had a solid basis for coming to them with this information. However, I didn't relay that comment.

I glanced over at my mom, who had a somber look on her face. My journal entry from that evening noted that my words to her were, "Mom, I don't know why, after 38 years, this is so important, but it is. I don't need or want another mom, if this decision concerns you.

You will always be my mom. I think you and Dad have a right to know this much. I will decide about the rest." At the time of my visit, my only intention was to tell my folks about my discovery and why I wanted to contact my birth mother. I wasn't sure if I would tell them how or when I might contact my birth mother.

I had a feeling Dad knew more about my adoption than he wanted to share that evening. He didn't seem surprised by anything I told them, but I didn't have enough information to ask him questions. He didn't ask, and I offered no additional explanations. Meanwhile, Mom appeared completely flabbergasted by everything I said. She told me she appreciated my initiative and understood my curiosity. I politely told her it didn't begin as a curiosity seeking venture; it was a God nudge.

Dad became very reflective, and we chatted for quite some time about the logistics of contacting my birth mother. His final words were, "You know what you need to do; just be careful."

I told him I appreciated his confidence in me and that I would think it through before proceeding. It felt like the end of the conversation and I needed to get home to be sure my children had gathered their school supplies together for the next day. Mom and Dad hugged me at the front door. Mom's embrace was longer and tighter than usual. I drew back, held her shoulders, looked into her eyes, and reminded her of my love and loyalty to her. She smiled as tears welled up in her eyes. I hugged her one last time, turned around, and walked down the front steps to the sidewalk leading to my car. On my drive home, I replayed our conversation and wondered if I should have said more, or if I had said enough. My eyes filled with tears. It had not been a difficult discussion, but it was an emotional one.

I arrived home and after the kids were all tucked in bed, I shared my conversation with my husband. He asked how I was going to proceed. He knew about the letter I had written my birth mother after I learned she lived in Lima. The letter read:

Dear Mrs. Morris,
I hope this letter comes at a good time for you. Please know that the only other person who is

aware of the contents of this is my husband.

I have made a one-month search to find my birth mother. I learned that my biological name was Bernice Anne Copeland. If my information is correct, my birth mother is Barbara Ann Copeland, who became Barbara Hasson, and is now known as Barbara Morris. I believe you are that woman.

I do not wish to upset you, but to thank you for giving me life. I have wonderful adoptive parents and am happily married with three healthy, amazing children. I feel so blessed.

I just wanted you to know how grateful I am to you. Every February 28th, I think of you. At my children's births, I thought of you. At each of their birthdays, and on Mother's Day I think of you.

Please understand that I don't want to interrupt or disturb your life. I will not write to you again, and I will make no other contact with you or the family members I have discovered during my research.

This is between the two of us. I am forever grateful for the decision you made in 1953-1954.

With deep appreciation,

Your daughter

I told my husband I was rethinking my current strategy of sending it through the mail. I knew she was married, and Ken Morris was probably not my biological father. What if her husband saw this letter, and she had never told him about me? Would that new information set into motion a wave of mistrust between these two people? Her other daughter was 18 months younger than me. Did this daughter know about me? Would it upset her to know she had a half or full-blooded sister? She was married and had two young children. How would this affect my birth mother and sister's relationship? Would that cause a problem of trust between them? How would I ever know whether she received the letter? There would be no return address on the envelope. I only wanted to say, "Thank you." I had not added the prospect of a meeting to the letter. So, if not the letter, what? I couldn't walk up to her house. That would have been rude and presumptuous.

The answer came quickly. On Tuesday, I had a transaction to make at the Credit Union, and Janine was behind the counter to assist me. As luck would have it, no one else was in the Credit Union. She asked how the search for my birth mother was progressing, and I gave her a quick recap of all that I had discovered. She asked if I'd decided what to do with this information. I described the letter and told her I didn't think the letter was the right way to approach my birth mother.

Janine left the counter, joined me in the lobby, gave me a hug, and offered to call Barbara on Wednesday if that was my wish. I didn't hesitate to tell her "yes, please." It seemed like the perfect solution to my dilemma. I gave Janine the contents of the letter to Barbara, and explained my reason for contacting her. As we discussed the process of providing Barbara with the information I had obtained, I advised Janine to give her my first name, but only if she asked. The purpose of the call was to thank Barbara; no other connection needed to be made. This was the thank you I thought God had in mind. She agreed and our plan was set. I felt a complete sense of relief as I drove home that afternoon.

Janine made the call after work on Wednesday evening, as discussed. I was on pins and needles as I imagined how that conversation might have played out. She had been through this experience herself as an adoptee, who contacted her birth mother. Her familiarity with this delicate set of circumstances and her tender spirit also made her the perfect choice. She called me immediately after the conversation.

She told me she introduced herself and said, "Mrs. Morris, please sit down. I have some happy news to share with you. I have a friend who was born on February 28, 1954, and she believes you are her birth mother. She said her birth name was Bernice Anne. Does that sound right to you?"

There was a pause, and a firm "Yes," from the other end. Janine told her of my desire to relay a message, simple in form, "thank you for giving her life. She is well and happy." They talked a bit more, and then Barb said, "Now, honey, you better sit down. My husband's funeral was fourteen days ago. It must be true that when God closes a door, He opens a window."

I'm certain the pause on Janine's end of the phone was longer than Barb's had been because neither Janine nor I were aware of that information.

As they continued their conversation, Janine went off script, asking if she would like to speak with me over the phone sometime. My birth mother said she would, but that she needed to discuss it with her other daughter before she made that decision. What a statement! I understood I was her daughter, but I had not been in her life for 38 years. She continued to recognize me as her daughter. That sentiment made me so happy.

I learned later about that evening when my birth mother and biological sister had a conversation about the call. Janine had told my birth mom which local high school I attended. My sister had attended the same high school and found two girls with my first name in her yearbook. She knew a bit about me, but not much about the other girl. In the end, she agreed that my birth mom should reach out to me.

I heard my birth mother's voice the following afternoon when she called me. Janine said her voice was soft, and she seemed kind. She was spot on. We were comfortable with each other from the start. I can't remember any moment when I wondered if my comments might be inappropriate, even though this was our first conversation.

We began with a conversation about Janine and her adoption. It was easy to segue into why I decided to allow her to make the call the previous evening, followed by a brief description of my journey to her. She asked several questions, but nothing too probing. Barbara was light-hearted and quick-witted. I learned she had an arsenal of jokes that were often used to add a bit of levity to a serious conversation. She asked about my family and seemed pleased to learn that I had a wonderful relationship with my parents. She verified that Bernard, Barney as she referred to him, was my biological father, solidifying the fact that Linda was my full-blooded sister. I asked about my sister and her family, which led her to ask about the ages of my children—her grandchildren. I told her I was sorry to hear about her husband's recent death, and she gave me a synopsis of their years together and his unexpected passing. After chatting for over an hour, we established a time to meet in her home on Saturday morning.

My journal entry noted that Friday was a "complete blur." After school, I pulled out my yearbook to find my sister's photo. It turned out that we attended the same high school, at the same time, for only one year. At first glance, she resembled my oldest son and daughter in the eyes. In the past, I thought they favored their father's side of the family. I was looking forward to a glimpse into my family's genes.

On Saturday morning, I paced back and forth in my bedroom as I decided which outfit looked best for meeting my biological mother for the first time. I understood it would be informal, but I had difficulty telling my mind not to worry about the details. After all, I wanted my end to go off flawlessly.

On May 2, 1992, I walked through the threshold of my biological mother's door and was greeted with a delightful smile and warm hug. She was the beautiful woman in the window on the day I had driven by her home. Her lovely appearance still surprised me. She was rather short and petite, nothing like the image I had of her in my mind's eye. She stood erect, and there was a familiarity about her that I couldn't explain. Perhaps I had brushed by her in the mall one day and we'd made eye contact.

She looked up at me as she spoke my name and smiled. I was nervous, but not giddy or tense. My journal entry simply said how elated I was to hear my birth mother's voice again, particularly when she said my name.

I've been told by several adoptees that one never forgets that first hug and who initiated it. It was definitely Barb, and I felt drawn in immediately. She led me from her immaculately maintained living room to a seat at her kitchen island, which became the hub of many long conversations. She offered me a cup of coffee, and I learned she liked her coffee dark, black and strong. She said she hoped I liked it that way, but she had already pulled creamer from her refrigerator since many had told her it was too strong. It was easy to imagine her serving others as a waitress, which had been her job for years. It was obvious she had prepared for this moment, too. Everything was within her arm's reach, and she was very comfortable in this setting.

As Barb sat down, our eyes met. I was so preoccupied listening to her directions about where to sit and answering questions about how I liked my coffee that I had not taken the time to really look at her. We smiled at the same time. Both of our eyes are green, hers with blue around the edges and mine with more of a hazel cast. Our eyelids, also, were very similar. I recognized those eyes, and seeing them on another's face, instead of in my bathroom mirror, caused me to shiver. Wow! There was someone in this world who I favored, if only a bit. As we chatted, I tried to memorize her face, her smile, and her laugh. It was all so new, yet oddly familiar.

On the counter, she had strategically placed a few newspaper articles and family photos that she was anxious to share with me. As I looked down at one of them, she gasped. I looked up, and she was smiling and said, "I can't deny you. You look just like your sister from the side." Her comment made me smile.

Barb's pets, Peaches and Pasha interrupted our conversation, momentarily. Peaches was a small white dog she had been caring for since her best friend's passing. Pasha was her beautiful German Shepherd. As she introduced them to me, I felt that connectivity one shares with like-minded individuals. She loved these dogs, and, at that moment, I knew we were "cut from the same cloth." My affection for all four-legged animals was extreme, and so was hers.

Barb was as interested in learning about my adoptive family as I was in knowing about my biological one. I was grateful for her interest. I brought along a carefully chosen collection of photos of my immediate family, and she politely listened to the stories about each one of them.

She wove her own stories into each newspaper article she showed me, and the details were deliberately generous. First was a local newspaper article about a serious accident that involved Barb and my sister, who had been in grade school at the time. Their car had collided with a train, and their injuries were significant. They both recovered, but it took a long, long time.

Next, she handed me a newspaper photo of her mother, my maternal grandmother, whose little league baseball team surrounded her. My grandmother was the first woman in Lima to serve as a Minor League baseball coach and the only woman manager in the Lima Boys Baseball League, a program in which 600+ young boys were involved. She offered to coach the Cougars in the Jaycee Division, since so many adult men were serving in WWII. The local paper had a picture of her seated, wearing a lovely short-sleeved summer dress and sandals while instructing her team. Clearly, she had their complete attention. Barb puffed up proudly as she remarked about how her mother's team won a second-place trophy that year.

The last article was regarding her dad, my granddad, who was actively involved in local government. He was the chairman of the Allen County Board of Elections for years. I sensed her deep admiration for him as she spoke of him so fondly. She showed me photos of him that were taken over the years. He passed away in 1981, eleven years before I met Barbara.

We spent most of the morning together. I was sorry that our time together seemed to fly by. We told each other how wonderful it was to meet and how we wanted to resume our conversation in the coming weeks. Barb said she would get in touch with my sister, Linda, and set up a time for the three of us to meet in Barb's home.

I left Barb's home that day feeling grateful for the opportunity to meet her and to be introduced to some of my biological family through photos and stories. Later that afternoon, I told my husband that I had a sense of peace and felt at ease in her presence.

It was the beginning of what would become countless conversations over cups of strong coffee in her home over the years. Seventeen years of getting to know one another, past and present. Despite our biological relationship, it developed like a typical friendship. It was slow at first; nothing rushed or contrived. We took our time getting to know one another. Because we lived in the same town, we had a great deal in common from the beginning. We loved our families and had a similar passion for animals, especially dogs. She was sincerely happy for my good fortune to have lived my life with the Lawson family.

We soon discovered we had to watch the clock during our visits.

It seemed we could have talked well into the night during those first visits, but there was never a sense of urgency to know the entire story.

On our first visit, there would be no deep dive into the topic of adoption. I made only one request: I asked if she and the rest of the family would keep our reunion private. We lived in a small town. My parents came first, and I wanted to be certain that the decision I made would not come back to haunt them. It was their decision to keep my adoption under wraps and I respected that.

That same day, I also asked my husband, George, to keep me in check regarding my attention to and my attitude toward my adoptive and biological families. Shiny new things have a way of enticing us to forget other things around us. Every aspect of my adoptive family seemed new, and exciting. Barb and I put our best selves forward at our initial meeting. Everyone and everything seemed wonderful. Never did I want my adoptive parents to take a back seat to my biological family, and I wanted George to be my watchman to help guard that priority.

As the years went by, I learned that individual members of both my biological and adoptive families would have opportunities to interact with one another, sometimes in occupational settings. To my knowledge, there was never a word spoken about the relationship my birth mother and I shared. George's sister was good friends with one of my biological grandmother's closest friends. Three months after I had met my grandmother, our youngest son was in a very serious car accident. George's sister called her friend to ask for prayer for his recovery. This friend began a prayer chain that included my biological grandmother. My grandmother didn't know she was praying for her great-grandson until he was home and well on his way to a complete recovery. This sister attended the same church as one of my biological aunts. Later, I would learn that the same aunt graduated from high school with George's eldest sister. Small town. Small world.

Two Saturdays after visiting Barb for the first time, I met my sister, Linda, and our unique and precious relationship began. There was an immediate connection and that same sense of familiarity. Initially, I noticed that some of our mannerisms and interests were similar. Our physical likeness was undeniable. Our fashion choice was similar, as were our hair styles. When we met for our first family gathering in early July 1992, we wore identical outfits; khaki shorts, a brown belt, and a white top.

Our conversation was very light and fun filled. There was never a lull in our exchange nor an uncomfortable moment that afternoon. After learning about each other's family, we talked about high school days and friends we might have known in common. We discovered we were very good friends with the same girl. She had been my neighbor and friend in grade school and Linda's good friend in high school.

At some point, I glanced at both my mom and my sister and thought just how fortunate I was to meet them in person rather than to have read about them in obituaries related to the car accident that occurred over thirty years earlier. Barb's leg had been badly injured and, initially, some thought she might not live because of her impactful injuries. Her road to recovery was long. Linda had sustained a severe head injury. Both were enjoying excellent health when I met them. The only apparent remnant of the accident was a metal pin placed in Barb's hip.

As our time came to a close, we discussed setting up another get-together during summer vacation. It had been a wonderful beginning. Perhaps our children would meet the next time. We could decide that at a later date. The three of us embraced, and I entered my car with a smile from ear to ear. I was so grateful for God's nudges and told Him so as I drove home.

When I opened the side door to my house, my husband was inside to greet me and ask how the visit went. I told him I felt very welcomed into their family of two. Happy and content seemed inadequate adjectives to describe how a special day like that should be perceived, but that was all I could articulate. My soul was content and at peace; my heart felt happy and grateful.

Several weeks later, I was introduced to my maternal grandmother, an aunt, uncle, and cousin in my grandmother's home. She welcomed me with a hug, and instantly I felt at ease and right at home. It was incredible to note that less than two months earlier, these individuals would have been strangers I passed on the sidewalk or bumped into in a grocery store or our local mall. I would not have noticed any similarity or reason to wonder about their identity. Contrast that with the notion of intimacy when in their presence the very first time. Perhaps, it's the "shiny new object" phenomenon, or the genealogical feeling of connectivity to one another.

In 1992, my sons were thirteen and sixteen years old and felt awkward about my adoption discovery. I told them about their biological grandmother shortly after she and I had met in her home. They listened to the stories, but they were not interested in participating in any of the gatherings. The weekend after I told Nate and Brian, I told their six-year-old sister, Hilly. She ran down the stairs to her brothers, yelling, "I know something you already know." We couldn't contain our laughter. She was so excited to share the news, but it sounded like she was informing them of something they didn't already know. That comment would make its way into many conversations over the years, mainly from her Grandma Morris (Barb). Our daughter was at the age to enjoy all of it, and relished the chance to get together with her other family whenever an opportunity arose.

Barb planned the next family gathering in her home on a warm and sunny Saturday afternoon in June. George and our daughter, Hilly, went with me. She enjoyed meeting Linda's children, who were close to Hilly's age. They connected quickly. I met my biological uncle and part of his family. My adoptive family was small, so having all these aunts and uncles might have seemed overwhelming, but it wasn't. My introduction to each one came gradually, and they showed grace when I forgot to whom they belonged.

During the rest of that year, I had opportunities to meet most of the family at several informal gatherings. It was exciting to see how much my children resembled my biological family. No DNA test was necessary to verify their ancestry; it was obvious from the start.

If it had ended there, I would have understood the meaning behind the God nudge and would have been grateful. But the blessings continued in the days, weeks, and years that followed. Layer upon layer of love and adventures transpired. They have not been without a few trials and some sleepless nights along the way, but they were entirely worth the risk.

Barb was accurate when she said, "When God closes a door, He opens a window." She said goodbye to her husband and hello to her first daughter. Those words touched my life, as well. God closed the door to the secret I felt the need to hide and opened the window to all the joy that was unearthed when this secret came to light.

—Chapter 5—

First Love

The secret associated with "the word, 'adopted'" affected Barb in much more challenging and burdensome ways than it did with me. She grew up in a modest home with two sisters, Marilyn, two years older—and Shirley, four years younger. Her brother, Larry, was ten years younger.

Barb was 15 years old when her mother and father divorced. The local newspaper published an article stating the date of their divorce. The year was 1947, and this article was probably noteworthy, not only because of the times, but also because my granddad had been a 1st ward councilman from 1942 to 1945. He was a public figure and might have had other political aspirations in the future. Whatever the reason behind the published article, the divorce shook up the family.

Over the years, family members told me that Barb exhibited a "feisty nature" as a youngster, and when she turned 16, she left home to live with her girlfriends. Her older sister had already left, married, and moved out of town. Barb chose to live close to her dad's downtown store, Copeland's Drug Store, which was in front of and attached to his ex-in-law's grocery, Bodiker's Market.

Barb became a waitress to pay her portion of the monthly bills. In late 1952, she met Barney, my biological father, who was already married. Their romance was exciting to Barb. During our visits, she told me stories about this special man and how much she had adored him. This gregarious, larger-than-life, forbidden, married man consumed her thoughts, which eventually guided her down the only path she would allow herself to follow: the path that led to the story of me.

She poured her love into him; he was all she desired and had never known before - a man who lavished her with compliments and gifts. She told me his carefree and fun-loving personality drew her in. He was 15 years older, drove a Cadillac, and smoked an expensive, sweet-smelling cigar. I believe she charmed him with her beauty, her captivating smile, and her ability to put him at ease with her contagious laugh and punchline-perfect jokes. They had an affair, an escape from their rather ordinary lives. She called him her first real love.

In May, 1953, my birth mother was twenty-one years old when she became pregnant with me. Barney had been married for nine years with children. He chose to stay with them, leaving Barb to navigate the waters of pregnancy by herself.

Barney passed away in 1990, two years before I felt led to thank Barb, so I will never know his side of this story.

Barb moved in with her younger sister, who rented one half of a side-by-side duplex. The girls' mother and stepfather lived in the other unit. They and her father were the only ones who were made aware of her condition. Barb held her secret and continued to work until she was almost six months pregnant, boarded a Greyhound bus, and was transported to an unwed mother's home in Columbus, ninety miles away.

In the 1950s through the early 70s, it was not uncommon for a single pregnant woman to be sent away from town so as not to "disgrace" her family. Sometimes, family members weren't told about the pregnancy. In fact, Barb's younger sister, with whom she lived, was told she had gone away to help care for her elderly aunt. Her sister told me she never questioned who the aunt was.

There were several unwed mother's homes in Ohio, with Florence Crittenton Home being the most recognized. However, Barb entered the Friends Rescue Home, where she would remain for the last three and a half months of her pregnancy. The Quakers managed and maintained this home.

Those months—from mid-November to the last day of February—must have been grueling for her. For the previous five years, she had lived on her own with very few rules. She worked hard and played even harder. She liked to smoke cigarettes, as did many her age in the 50s. She enjoyed going out with her friends on the weekends. The Home didn't permit smoking or drinking alcohol. Once, she told me she was probably in her best health while carrying me. She had to abide by their rules if she wanted to remain there. She had no money saved, and her parents were barely scraping by financially. Her mother and stepfather had two children under twelve and her father was single.

I can only speculate as to the financial arrangement made for my birth mom's stay at the Home. In 1955, a Columbus Dispatch article written to commemorate the Friends Rescue Home's 50th anniversary noted the total cost for an unwed mother's entire stay was $200.

My birth father remained silent during the last three and a half months of Barb's pregnancy with me. Barb had no communication with him. Until the day she signed documents releasing me to the State of Ohio's foster care system, Barb believed Barney would ride up, like a knight in shining armor, and sweep her off her feet as he had during their romantic interlude. Even my birth certificate is a hope-filled connection to him by naming me Bernice Anne.

Instead, I entered the world on a frigid Sunday afternoon at 12:46 P. M. Barb had begun having labor pains the evening before. As she described it, my birthday began with a short, uncomfortable night and a long, painful morning. She told me she remembered the nurse had to remind her to grab the handrail as she slowly descended one flight of stairs to the labor and delivery room, where she would remain until the following afternoon. In the daylight, she observed icicles hanging from the eaves, just outside the second floor windows of her room.

As her labor continued, she recalled the nurse updating her as the weather transitioned from sleet to light snow, to a drizzle, and ended with fog as she drifted off. She knew nothing about what to expect. No one had prepared her for this excruciating experience, and she was then unaware of much going on around her, only the discomfort within her. Barb delivered me alone, except for the professionals caring for her on that last day of February. Despite the damp, cold conditions outdoors, she awoke to a warm fireplace in the five-bed recovery room on the second floor. She was the only one in the room, and the nurse brought me to her for a short visit. She recalled her initial response was to unwrap the blanket to check my fingers and toes—all normal.

That woke me up, which didn't surprise me when she told me. I still like to be warm and bundled up in the winter. She remembered a brief look into my eyes before I drifted off to sleep. The nurse came back within what she said seemed like fifteen or twenty minutes. She told Barb it was time to say her goodbyes to me. Tears welled up in her eyes but she said nothing. She kissed my cheek and handed me back to the nurse. The nurse whisked me away to the nursery, and Barb rested her weary body in the convalescing-recovery room. That would be the last time she saw me for over 38 years. It wasn't long before she fell asleep, this time for much of the afternoon. One of the Home's staff members took me to St. Ann's Hospital that day, or the following one.

Barb remained in the convalescing room until the day they released her to go back home. She would never have to ascend that last flight of stairs to the third-floor dormitory again. Five days later, a nurse escorted her down the two flights of stairs, where her small suitcase of belongings was waiting for her beside the front door. One employee retrieved the station wagon, picked her up in front of the house, and took her to the bus stop just down the street, where she boarded the Greyhound for home.

A court-appointed case worker had picked me up at the hospital two days earlier. We took the same route and arrived in the same town as my mother. The case worker placed me in the arms of my foster parents, who would become my adoptive parents eight months later.

After she fully recovered from my delivery, my birth mother convinced her younger sister to move with her to another town where their older sister lived with her family. She wanted a fresh start away from the man who no longer wanted her in his life, or so she thought. They found employment quickly and shared the apartment expenses.

However, that arrangement didn't last long because Barney found her and their relationship rekindled. What began as a first love had a second movement, and they continued their love affair. She became pregnant by him a second time and moved back home. Three months before delivering their second daughter, Barney divorced his wife and married Barb. Sadly, their relationship remained tumultuous. By September of the following year, Barney left again and reunited with his former wife, with whom he would remain until his death, thirty-three years later.

Closed adoptions were commonplace in the 50s. Barb's secret was two-fold: a mysterious pregnancy and a private adoption. She never told me how it felt to come back home without a baby in her arms after carrying me for nine months. I thought talking about it might stir up unhappy memories, or make her feel she had to explain more than she wished to share, so I never asked. Several studies, which began in the 1950s, concluded that a degree of prenatal attachment exists between a mother and her baby during and after birth. Separation, either through death or adoption/foster care can be psychologically upending when this type of bonding occurs. According to several studies, aspects of the bond between these entwined lives endure. How difficult it must be for the birth mother to experience both postpartum depression and separation anxiety.

It is undeniable: adoption affects everyone it touches, perhaps, no one more than the unwed mother. There was no manual to navigate the waters of adoption in the 50s. No counselor or social worker explained to the birth mother how to handle the potential questions and discussions, the controversial viewpoints she might encounter, or the defense she had for her decision. It was a matter of paddling through the system with the limited connections available, treading the rough waters of pregnancy in mental isolation, and doggy paddling back home with a heavy heart and a traumatized body. Disappointment, regret, or guilt do not automatically disappear just because you're back home with family.

How does one endure the trauma of relinquishing her baby and disassociating herself from the short-term relationships forged with other unwed mothers at the Home? My mother was advised to leave behind any association with those she met while in the Home. Cut all ties and connections. Go back to your 'new' life with your family. How does one begin again as if nothing has happened while remaining quietly complacent with the conversations about Aunt "so and so," and her recovery? My mom must have carried an unimaginable weight of emotions home with her.

When Barb and I first met in April 1992, we were still a bit wet behind our ears, damp from unresolved questions related to the "word," and feeling relatively isolated for thirty-eight years. We rarely spoke of it with anyone. I wondered about the why of it all, and she wondered about where I had gone and who had raised me. Other questions tugged at our heartstrings, as well. We were fortunate to resolve some questions swirling around in our heads for years. We agreed that the silence and faint whispers following a closed adoption were stifling, and sometimes we struggled to live with the "word" attached to us.

My biological parents' love may not have endured; it may have been messy. However, it created two human beings who care deeply for others and each other.

It generated an enduring love whose ripple effects have touched three generations… and counting.

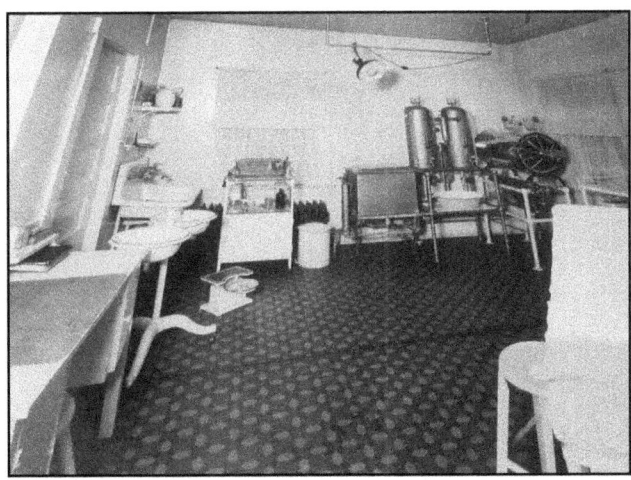

Ohio Yearly Meeting of Friends. (1933). Labor and Delivery room. [photograph]. Friends Rescue Home annual fundraising brochure. (p. 3). (Photo copied with permission from the Archives Committee of Malone University and representatives from EFC-ER.)

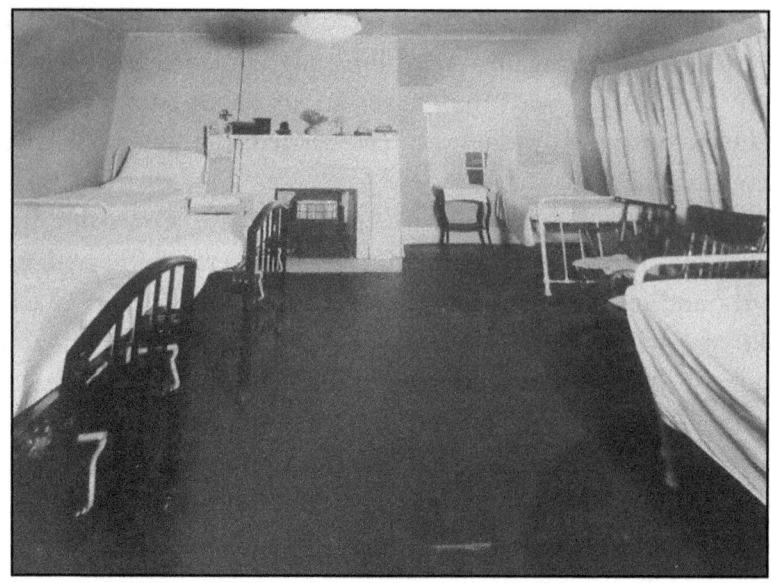

Ohio Yearly Meeting of Friends. (1933). Recovery and Convalescing Room. [photograph]. Friends Rescue Home annual fundraising brochure. (Photo copied from a FRH pamphlet with permission from the Archives Committee of Malone University and representatives from EFC-ER.) (p. 4).

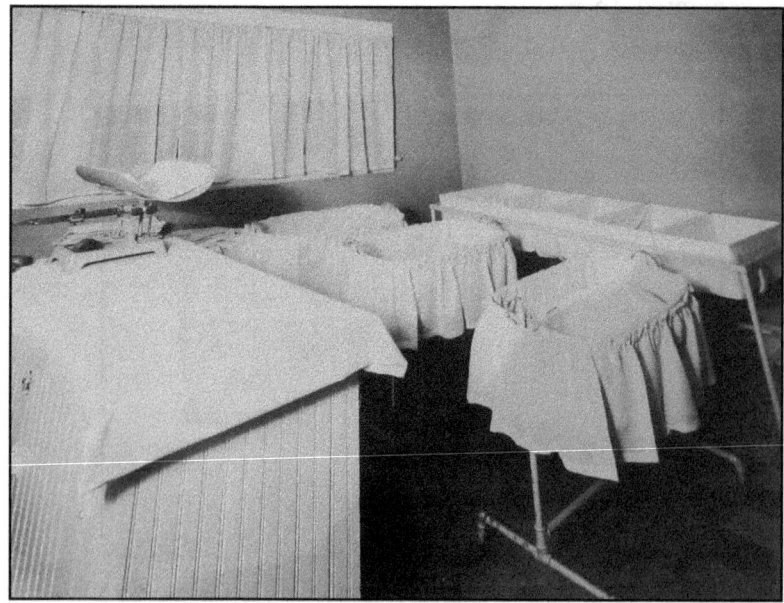

Friends Rescue Home. (1936). Baby Nursery. [photograph]. Friends Rescue Home annual fundraising brochure. (Photo copied with permission from the Archives Committee of Malone University and representatives from EFC-ER.) (p. 4).

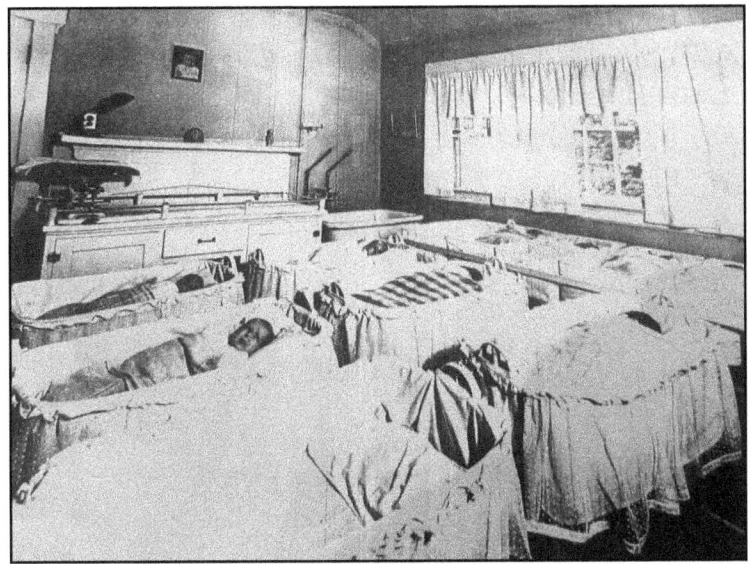

Ohio Yearly Meeting of Friends. (1936). Baby Nursery. [photograph]. Friends Rescue Home annual fundraising brochure. (Photo copied with permission from the Archives Committee of Malone University and representatives from EFC-ER.)

—Chapter 6—
Birth Mom

Getting acquainted with my birth mother was like putting on one's favorite warm, well-fitting sweater that wraps you in comfort during the long winter months in northwest Ohio. From the moment we met, she let me into her world without the slightest hesitation. If she held back any information, it was to respect another person's privacy. We agreed that was the best way to proceed when our conversations led to stories about our families. From the beginning, I was keenly aware of the fact that not everyone has a positive reunion experience, and I didn't presume to believe that ours would remain so in the years to follow. From the beginning, I held her in high regard, and remained mindful of our delicate connection each time we were together.

After our first meeting in Barb's home, I called her at least twice a month. She chose not to contact me in case my adoptive parents were in my home visiting. However, in the event of an emergency, she knew I would make myself available for her right away.

We met in her home at least once a month for years. We would begin by swapping animal stories, clearly understanding we shared a strong passion for them. Initially, we spent much of our time learning about each other's family and the years leading up to our meeting. When I met each family member, I gathered more history, and soon we were building memories of our own. During the fall, we watched at least one college football game together, and began our own traditions related to Thanksgiving and Christmas. In the winter, we talked for hours about our favorite basketball teams and celebrated our winter birthdays together. In the spring and summer I loved sitting in her backyard, listening to her talk about all of her lovely flowers and enjoying her frequent feral, four-legged friends that she showered with their favorite treats. Of course, much of the time was spent catching up on each other's lives since our last conversation.

Occasionally, I drove Barb down to Columbus to visit my sister and her family. Typically, the day included a special school, or church event, involving one of Linda's children. From time to time, we went to Barb's mother's home for a visit, or she would join us in Barb's kitchen.

One day Barb, Linda and I went to the local Cracker Barrel restaurant together. It was our first public outing, and we smiled at each other when the waitress approached us and asked if Linda and I were sisters. It was such a quick observation, and we were befuddled. We fumbled for the right words as it was the first time someone had inquired. Our similarity was obvious, but the fact we had never imagined having a sister for over 37 years, it was special that a stranger asked us. After that encounter, we decided our response should be that we were classmates in high school, which was a true statement.

That first year went by so quickly. The following year was my oldest son's senior year of high school. Two years later, it would be my younger son's turn to graduate. Our twelve-year-old daughter was involved in her own activities. Our family's schedule was busy, but staying connected with Barb remained a priority.

She came to our house on two occasions; once for a Christmas gathering including my grandmother and my sister and her family, and once to meet our new puppy. We invited her into our home on multiple occasions over the years, but Barb preferred to entertain in the comfort of her home.

My biological family assembled for summer reunions, birthday and anniversary celebrations, and Christmas Eve was spent in my Grandma Grouver's home. My husband and I attended many of the gatherings, but not the one on Christmas Eve. Instead of attending, I began a tradition of taking a pumpkin roll to her home for that evening. My husband was a shift worker, which meant his schedule for resting fluctuated. We were very mindful of that, especially over the holidays, because it was important to be completely present for his family and my adoptive family's celebrations the following day. On several Christmas Eves, I stopped by to deliver the pumpkin roll to Grandma Grouver's home before the gathering. Barb and I developed the traditions of exchanging Christmas gifts the week before Christmas.

I called Barb on our birthdays. On my second birthday after we met, she brought up my adoption and what had transpired during that time in her life in greater detail than ever before. The day we met, she made it clear that I had the freedom to ask her about it anytime. After that birthday, I chose to wait until my birthday to ask any particularly significant questions. As soon as I got off the phone or back home, I added that part of our conversation to my journal entry for the day.

As our relationship gradually developed, so did the way I addressed my birth mother. Before I knew her, I called her my birth mom or biological mom in conversations with my closest friends. Never just Mom. In the first years of our relationship, I referred to her as Barb in her presence, or Grandma Morris when with my children. When my sister and I were together, I referred to her as our mom.

When we met, Barb signed cards, "Barbara." I don't recall ever calling her that in her presence. However, some of her friends and family did. Most members of my family would refer to her as "Barb", or "your mother." I was comfortable with either.

After her mother, Grandma Grouver, died in 2003, Barb signed all of her cards to me with the name "Mom." I followed suit and addressed her as "Mom" in all the cards I would send to her. In her presence, I began calling her "Mom" as often as I called her Barb.

It wasn't until a few months after my adoptive mother, Mom Lawson, died I realized I was addressing Barb as Mom all the time. I'm still not sure why. Mom Lawson was Mom Lawson when I spoke with others outside the Lawson family. I suppose it felt natural for me to refer to her as Barb instead of Mom because of my strong sense of respect for Mom and Dad Lawson. They were and will remain Mom and Dad. I don't believe I disrespected Mom Lawson's memory by referring to Barb as my mother, because both of them were.

Two of my favorite memories occurred when Barb was in the presence of her first great-grandson, Jacob, our oldest son's child. Jacob never met his Great-Grandpa Lawson because he passed a month after Jacob's birth. Although Dad Lawson was 87 years old, we were unaware of any significant health issues, so there wasn't a sense of urgency in their meeting immediately after his birth. None of us suspected they wouldn't meet or have time to get acquainted. When Jacob was just one month old, he met his Great-Grandma Lawson in the nursing home where she resided after Dad Lawson's passing. Mom Lawson was so weak that she could only hold him for a short time. It was the only time I saw her smile that Christmas. Sadly, that would be their first and only meeting.

Barb and Jacob met when he was 10 months old. He and his family lived ninety miles away and he was in my care for several days. One day, while he was taking his afternoon nap, I called Barb to see if she would like to meet him later in the afternoon. Her reply was, "Of course I do!" I talked to him about his great-grandmother from the moment I buckled him into his car seat until our arrival at her front doorstep.

Barb greeted us with a huge smile when she opened the door. Their eyes met, and it was love at first sight. She delighted him with a musical toy dog and delicious cookies. She would have done almost anything to make him smile, but her fun-loving personality was all that was needed to keep him giggling and happy. Everything he did was wonderful to her, and she made sure he knew it. I have a picture of them seated by her fireplace locking eyes and smiling. I'm not sure who was more enamored. It was as if time stood still, and my presence was certainly not required. They entertained one another for over an hour, and I hated to see their time together come to a close. When I picked him up to leave, he reached out to her for a hug. She willingly obliged, and I was on the verge of tears as they embraced while he remained in my arms.

As much as I hoped there would be many more embraces in their futures, there was only one more meeting. A few weeks after Jacob turned three, he came to stay with us for a few days. I arranged for him to visit with his great grandmother early one morning, and they reconnected in much the same way as they had the first time. She was prepared for him, and their playful energy generated more smiles and laughter. However, it was short lived because her health had deteriorated, and she needed an oxygen tank to sustain her. We didn't stay long, but it was sweet. Barb passed away a month after their reunion. I wish they'd had more time together, but not living in the same town, his parent's work schedules, and a busy, hard-to-determine toddler's schedule had to be taken into consideration. He had the privilege of meeting and playing with his great-grandma and they had the best time together.

My journals contain the years of memories with Mom. However, there will always be unanswered questions that tug on my heartstrings now that she's gone. We can't possibly know the entirety of another's life, only the essence. I will always treasure the knowledge I received from Barb, as well as the love we shared during the precious time we had together.

—Chapter 7—
Adoptive Parents

My adoptive parents met at a United Service Organization sponsored canteen dance in 1942. Dad was in the army and stationed at Chanute Field, near Rantoul, Illinois. Mom lived nearby in Clinton, Ill. She was the baby of the family and quite pretty. While in high school, she was crowned Miss Clinton. When they met, she was twenty-two years old and a USO junior hostess, which meant she and her peers were given the task of making the servicemen feel at home while away from home. During World War II, this organization hosted dances for the troops at various mobile USO sites and other locations. The hostesses served food and drinks, and danced with the servicemen. While getting to know one another that evening, they discovered they shared the same birthdate, however Mom was always quick to point out that she was a year younger.

It must have been love at first sight because they were quickly engaged and subsequently married on March 20, 1943. However, not everyone was excited about their marriage. My dad's mom had other plans for her oldest child and only son. He was moving up the ranks in the army, and she was certain her bright and ambitious son would return home and complete his Juris Doctor degree at Ohio State University, thanks to President Franklin D. Roosevelt's G.I. bill for World War II veterans who wished to receive a college education.

She had a sweet girl in mind for him when he got back home. Those plans had to change because her son was already smitten by my mother. On many of their wedding anniversaries, Dad would delight in lavishly praising his "Miss Clinton" with a sweet poem. Afterward, he always remarked that there were those who said theirs was a hasty war marriage that would never last.

As the years passed, we would giggle at that ludicrous statement. We never asked who "those" people were. My brother Walt and I added that phrase "theirs was a hasty war marriage that would never last" to their blue marble bench which sits above their resting place. It was so ironic considering they were happily married for sixty-three years. Later, we learned from Dad's sister that those were his mother's words after learning they were getting married. Imagine our surprise and delight, simultaneously. Surprised to learn that Grandma Lawson was "those" people, and delighted that our dad, who revered his mother, would bring it up every year. At that moment, we believed Dad's comment was a compliment to his bride. Innocently, we took it a step further by placing that phrase on their bench.

They conceived my brother within the first month following their marriage. My parents were thankful for a full-term birth to avoid speculation and gossip. Walt III was born on January 11, 1944, in Riverside, California, the base where Dad was stationed with the army. After Dad's discharge, he began studying for his law degree, while the young family lived in the converted attic bedroom in his parents' home, in Columbus, Ohio.

My aunt told me that my adoptive mom changed during those years. She became very independent and strong-willed in order to stand up to my grandmother, who thought their marriage would never last. I didn't come along until ten years later, so I only knew my mom as an outspoken woman with a mind of her own. She was fearless, spoke her mind and put others in their place without hesitation. As much as I loved her and her spunky personality, I wish I had known her during the innocent time of their courting, early marriage and motherhood. I wonder if our personalities might have been more aligned. Instead, I was a quiet and reserved child. Before I was old enough to attend school, Mom would often sit alone reading a book in the living room, while I played with toys in my bedroom, alone. I rarely had a playmate. It was a different era, and my mom's focus was on making sure I grew up to be a respectful young lady. I wasn't confrontational, even in my teens.

On the other hand, my brother challenged nearly every rule that came down the pike. He was a smart, inquisitive boy, always wanting to push the boundaries just to see how far our folks would bend. As I saw it, his witty, confrontational personality was very similar to our mother's, and mine seemed more like our dad's. Dad was mild-mannered and always saw the glass as half full.

After law school, the family of three moved to Lima, Ohio. Dad, and a very good friend he had met in law school, began their law practice, while becoming increasingly involved in the community. He was a charter member of several civic groups and held positions on the boards of many others. They attended church regularly and Mom stayed home while raising Walt, as many women did in those years. She participated in various lady's organizations and church guilds. She had difficulty delivering my brother and wasn't able to conceive another child.

At some point, they scheduled an appointment to meet with their doctor to discuss an adoption. In the 1950s, a family entrusted their general practitioner to understand the health and well-being of his/her patient and the family, and he either advised them or agreed with their plan to adopt.

In the '50s, there were no assisted reproductive technologies, so in vitro fertilization or intrauterine insemination (IUI), cryopreservation, embryo donation (with gestational carriers) were not options. Nor was freezing embryos.

I became their child as much as my brother, their biological son. I can say, without reservation, they loved me unconditionally as long as they lived. I was their daughter. It didn't matter that I entered the world from another woman's womb, or that I didn't particularly look like anyone in the family. I was tethered to their hearts.

Mom Lawson never wished to discuss my adoption. In fact, she proudly told her friends, who she came to know later in life, that she was only in the hospital twice, and that was to give birth to her children.

When I was older, this would make me feel very uncomfortable to hear. The "word" changed from a secret to a lie. Subconsciously, I think I needed to know that she loved me, so I would never broach the topic of two hospitalizations, and only asked her about my adoption once. I was a young teenager, and the two of us were having a conversation about my cousin's birth father, who I never knew.

It seemed like the perfect time to inquire, so I awkwardly asked if she knew anything about the woman who gave birth to me. She said the only thing she knew was that the birth father was a businessman, who was married, he'd had an affair with his secretary, and I was born in a Columbus hospital. That was it. Nothing more asked and nothing more said. That was probably the reason I was not more inquisitive. Looking back, I imagine the abruptness of her comment was the reason I never talked with her about it again. It was the first time that it registered in my mind that my life was not an open book; some chapters were unavailable. My life was wonderful, and I felt deeply loved. I had no desire to "find" the rest of me. My family was decided years ago, and I need not look back, but keep moving in a forward direction. This was my thinking as a teenager.

God blessed my parents with long, full lives. My Dad enjoyed good health into his early 80s. He endured several procedures in his last years and died of a sudden heart attack when he was eighty-seven years old. He went to work on a Friday and died on Monday morning in his home. It was just the way he would have planned it.

When he passed, at eighty-seven years old, many of his clients were in shock as they walked through the line at the funeral visitation. They could not imagine life without him. He had been their counselor, legal advisor and friend. They had never noticed his aging. He often said: "As long as I have my mind and good vision, I can practice the profession that I love." I suppose they believed him invincible. I would have to admit that for a very long time, I did too.

At the time of his passing, my mom was eighty-six years old, and hospitalized due to multiple health concerns. Years earlier, she'd attended water aerobic exercise classes in the local YWCA pool and walked around the YW track at least twice a week. The year she turned eighty-three, she fell down the marble stairs at the YW, and the injuries she sustained that day would plague her for the rest of her life. Before Dad's passing, she was in tremendous back pain, her ability to walk was erratic, and what we thought were occasional TIA's caused her more problems. Her doctor recommended hospitalization to perform several tests, assess her current condition, and come up with a plan for her rehabilitation. She was supposed to be transported to a local nursing home for rehab on the day my dad died. Instead, the hospital graciously allowed her to remain there several extra days in order to build up her strength to endure her husband's visitation, funeral and burial. Thanks to the hospital's van and driver, Mom attended the evening visitation. I'm not sure she was really "present" because of the comments she made from time to time. The line of people was very long and everyone wanted to speak with her. I'm certain she was mentally, emotionally and physically drained.

The following week, Mom left the hospital and entered the rehab facility Dad had planned to admit her to just one week earlier. The facility was housed in a local convalescent home. Rehab didn't go well because her worst issue was a broken heart and they couldn't fix that. Less than three months later, my brother, sister-in-law and my husband surrounded Mom's bed as she breathed her last breath. I remember looking up at my brother and our tear-filled eyes met. We knew in our minds that this would be the likely outcome, but it still felt unimaginable that it was happening so quickly. The death certificate accurately stated her death was due to her "failure to thrive." She could not imagine herself thriving without the man who had loved her so well for over sixty-three years.

"Theirs was a hasty war marriage that would never last!" Grandma Lawson was proven wrong this time.

I had the privilege of knowing my adoptive parents for fifty-three years. They gave me all the tools I would need to navigate through life. They loved me and provided a safe place for me to thrive. I once said Dad was my compass. I could count on him for every answer, or a direction in which to find the answer I couldn't discern. Mom gave me the gift of learning to cope with what life throws at me. As a youngster, she comforted me when I needed it, but more often she advocated for me until I could advocate for myself. My brother's love was also steadfast. Our ten-year age gap evaporated when I became an adult. There was a mutual respect that kept us close, in spite of the vast distance between our personalities and our street addresses over the years.

Mom and Dad accomplished many things in their lifetimes, but to me their legacy will be how they unapologetically demonstrated unconditional love for me during our years together. They were not perfect, but they loved me perfectly. I am sincerely grateful that God chose this family for me. I am truly blessed to be a Lawson.

—Chapter 8—
The Trifold

Fifteen years after I'd first held my original birth certificate in my hands, my curiosity was rekindled. In 2007, the year my adoptive mom passed away, I became the executor of my folks' estate. The idea of cleaning out their home of forty-seven years was daunting. Walt suggested I prepare the home for its eventual sale while he continued to operate Dad's law practice, which he had joined ten years prior to Dad's death.

Thus began my year-long schedule of working at our county's high school Alternative Program during the week and heading over to our folks' house to clean out, clean up, and reminisce on Saturdays. I discovered ways to cope with my sadness while sifting through their belongings and attempting to remain focused. I knew the contents of their house like the proverbial back of my hand. After all, I lived in this dwelling from the time I was six until college.

After college and marriage, my husband and I lived in the same town and celebrated most holidays and special occasions in my family's home. No surprises were anticipated. My method would be to start with a difficult, sometimes sad, room or area of the house. I'd organize and file the items according to their destination. Five totes were labeled for each of the grandchildren, alongside a tote labeled for my brother and one for me. Additionally, there were black garbage bags for things no one wanted or could use. Boxes were lined up against the wall for several charities.

When I was losing steam or focus, I found areas of the house that I knew would bring a smile to my face. One such place was the sunroom, where the baby grand piano sat from the time I was old enough to play it. There were lovely, large windows on three sides of the room, and it was where I fell in love with playing the cello. Happy memories. On one side of the room, there were built-in window seats with hinged tops that one could lift and place items inside. For years, I had accumulated piano and cello sheet music, and looking back at them brought fond memories of my youth.

The day I chose to open the window seat storage, I was surprised by what was not in there. As a youngster in the 60s, I was enamored with all the Kennedys. Camelot was like a dream to me until President Kennedy was assassinated. Then his brother, Bobby, was killed. It broke my heart to watch their family's grief, which was shown on all the television networks, as well as displayed within every newspaper and periodical in our home for weeks. I saved every single article in the window seats. I recall gathering them up to use for reference in a sociology research paper in college. I took care to bring all the information home and placed it in a paper bag from the local grocery. I added it to all the sheet music and assumed it was still there. To my befuddlement, only the sheet music remained. All the periodicals and newspapers were gone. I looked around the room, under the window seat pillows and the small bookshelf in the corner of the room. They were nowhere to be found. I sat at the piano bench, and instead of crying, I began laughing uncontrollably. My mom despised the Kennedys with a passion. She was a staunch Republican, and we could not talk about them in our house because it always caused an uproar. She had, in her vernacular, "pitched" all the reminders of the Kennedy family. "Good riddance" would have been her mental comment. I had to laugh.

After she had disposed of these items, I imagined her briskly wiping her hands together as if the printed materials had some power to leave a stain on her. On a separate occasion, when Mom was in her early 80s and unable to go up and down the stairs in her home, I recall going up to her bedroom to retrieve an item from her dresser. Much to my delight, I noticed old letters with familiar handwriting tied together in a bow with an old, tattered red and white ribbon! They were war letters written to my mom from my dad. How excited I was to scurry down the stairs to show them to her. The annoyed expression on her face told me she was not pleased as I handed them to her. I was rarely addressed by my first and middle name. That was saved for the moments when I was being disciplined. I'll not forget her words or the way she looked at me while saying them. "Janice Adele, you are not to look at those letters until I am long gone. Do you hear me?"

Of course, "Yes, ma'am," was my immediate verbal response, and taking them straight back to their previous location was the only appropriate action. I made a mental note of where they were as I gently placed them in the back of her dresser drawer.

It was on a particularly difficult day when I remembered the letters and climbed the stairs to their bedroom. To my complete amazement, when I opened the dresser drawer, they were not there. In their place were lovely handkerchiefs that she enjoyed placing in her pocketbook. They were spotless and rarely used.

Weeks passed before the mystery of the missing love letters was divulged as I cleared out Mom's well-organized clothes closet. She enjoyed her large shoe collection, and each pair was tucked away in its original box. Her closet floor was completely filled - three rows deep and three rows high. In the back row, in the bottom box, and all the way at the end of the closet, I found the forbidden letters in a Clarks shoe box. I laughed until I cried. I had no idea how she fit those letters in that box; perhaps she had nicely asked her daily caregiver, who had become a good friend, to hide them. I know Dad would not have been able to perform such a feat. As of late, he was having difficulty bending over, and he surely would not have gotten down on the carpeted floor because he knew assistance would be needed to stand back up. He knew better than to take that chance.

However the "cover-up" was executed, it was done with great forethought, and I had to applaud her ingenuity. As I poured through the lovely poetic prose with my dad's mastery of the written word, I began to understand her disdain for my ever-laying eyes on them before she was "long gone." The thought of my daughter reading love letters, like those composed by my dad for my mother during the war, would have disturbed me, too.

On another day, I was unpacking my dad's dresser drawers and became unimpressed with what I discovered. I started at the bottom and pulled out his old sweaters, many of which had multiple holes or stains. Moving up to the next drawer, there was sleepwear along with white undershirts and t-shirts. The drawer above it contained more undergarments and socks. But the prize was about to be uncovered in one of the top, side-by-side drawers. On the left-hand side were lots of perfectly pressed handkerchiefs, along with a plethora of pins from all the civic organizations of which he was a member. I found old watches from his dad, as well as his special cologne that I spent more than a bit of time inhaling. Carefully, I set out all the military pins before adding them to a box marked "Grandpa's army pins." He had so many army relics to be distributed to those interested in them. I was getting tired but determined to empty the contents of his dresser that day. In the right-hand side drawer, I found old and faded photos of him with Mom, several mementos from his college days at Ohio State University, and postcards and pamphlets from various places they had visited over the years. My dad was a paper keeper, which was consistent with his profession as an attorney, I suppose.

He saved special maps from his time in WWII and the Korean conflict, as well as pamphlets from the places he and Mom had traveled together. They'd had a movie camera and a small point-and-shoot camera, but they rarely took them on their trips. I could appreciate these pamphlets as windows into what mattered most in his life. There were so many stacks of "important" papers piled up in the nooks and crannies of their home that it had become common practice for me to toss them into the wastebasket. I decided these must be more important since they were in his dresser drawer.

I pored over each one of them, trying to recall the year and their significance. It was then that I discovered the real prize. There in the palm of my hand lay a golden-colored, trifold pamphlet with the words FRIENDS HOME - A home for unwed mothers. Underneath the words was a picture of a large, elegant, stone home. Beneath the picture was written the same address as the one that appeared on my original birth certificate - 245 North Powell Ave., Columbus, Ohio. The only difference between my original birth certificate and this trifold was the name; my birth certificate read Friends Rescue Home, and this document called it Friends Home.

My hands started shaking; my heart was racing. My tired body and weary mind were re-energized as I quickly read the pamphlet in my hands. Tears rolled down my cheeks when I imagined my Dad's reaction while reading it. How had he acquired it? Did he save it after a church presentation where donations were requested, or had a colleague handed it to him elsewhere? They were always attending fund-raisers for missions and missionaries on Sunday evenings at our church. However, perhaps their doctor had the pamphlet in his office for those wishing to adopt. How he acquired it didn't matter. It was a piece of my life puzzle that fit.

The pamphlet's contents included a description of the services provided, which covered residential care, health supervision, educational programming, counseling services, and recreational opportunities. All were outlined with bullet points. I'm sure Dad appreciated these added details. There were photos of several pregnant women, but only from the side or behind their backs. One mother-to-be was seated in a chair listening to another playing the piano, while others were playing a game around a table in a large living room. Another photo, taken in a dormitory, showed two women sitting on a bed close together, facing away from the camera. These photos provide clear evidence that their privacy was respected. No full-face images.

The fifth page contained descriptions of the purpose of the home, its organization, where it received its support, and the fees charged. It read: "Friends Home has existed to serve the needs of unwed mothers since 1905, providing professional help for their physical needs and skilled guidance for their spiritual needs." In the early 1950s, this Ohio Yearly Meeting of Friends pamphlet stated: "the Home believes it is a character-building institution and has a responsibility to help the troubled find a new way of life."

Under Organization, it read: "An eleven-member Board of Trustees, appointed by the Ohio Yearly meeting of the Friends Church, is responsible for the operation of Friends Home. The staff includes a superintendent, two housemothers, two nurses, cook, housekeeper, laundress, and superintendent of grounds. An Advisory Council composed of carefully selected leaders from the business, professional and religious segments of the community is available for consultation on matters related to their specialties."

Under Support and Fees read: "Friends Home receives support from Ohio Yearly Meeting of Friends. It is a member agency of the United Appeal of Franklin County and also receives contributions from interested persons and organizations. Reasonable fees are paid by those served, or by others on their behalf, to help cover medical and residential care. Specific information about the fees currently in effect will be furnished on request. A plan for payment may be arranged with the Superintendent of the Home."

Fascinating. I would spend hours looking through the pamphlet, imagining different scenarios regarding the topic of an adoption that might have taken place between my mom and dad. I did know that the Home where I was born was never discussed. Mom had no idea I was born in the Home. She'd told me I was born in St. Ann's Hospital, in Columbus, Ohio.

I added the Friends Home pamphlet to my collection of information regarding my adoption and went back to complete the task of cleaning out the home where I'd grown up.

*

I enjoyed two more years with my birth mother after my adoptive mother died. On several occasions, Barb told me about the Friends Home. During one of my birthday conversations, when I felt the most comfortable asking her about what led up to my birth, I inquired about the place where I was born. She told me several stories and indulged me for a while. When I asked if she would ever want to revisit the place if it were still standing, she replied with an emphatic "NO!"

She added that she had no desire to go back to "reminisce." It had not been a happy place for her. She felt stifled and judged. The image she painted was that of a wretched place where unmarried, pregnant girls and women were warehoused and browbeaten into godly submission. The Quaker traditions and faith meant nothing to her. It was her opinion the Friends/Quaker women only saw her as a vessel carrying a child. Every day, she was reminded of the importance of her body remaining healthy and strong for the sake of the baby taking up residence within her and her eventual exodus from the Home. The food she was given, the household chores she was required to perform, and the scheduled daily walks around the property were all purposeful acts.

Her secret would remain safe as long as her figure remained comparable to her appearance when she left her hometown three and one-half months earlier. Traveling Quaker ministers and their wives held weekly services in the community living room, always reminding my birth mother of her "grievous sin." She was not able to hear them talk to her about Christ's redemptive love. Only God's wrath and judgment came through to her, and it was loud and clear. While at the home, she was not interested in hearing anything other than the footsteps of her lover. That would not happen.

When I met my birth mother, she had given her life to Christ, and His redemptive love was obvious. By her own admission, she was a changed woman. She took ownership of her past but was not stuck in it. She gave generously to others, in her prayer life as well as providing food for those in need. She read her Bible and graciously shared the verses of encouragement she'd learned: never pushy or judgmental, just caring. One could not leave her house without being offered something to take home. Once a week, she volunteered at a soup kitchen and financially gave to those in need when she saw an opportunity.

One afternoon, she shared two highlights from her three and one-half month "incarceration." Her favorite was a visit with her older sister, Marilyn. She was her only visitor during those long, arduous months away from Home. She and Marilyn had always been close. They were two years apart in age but rarely separated when they were growing up. I've been told that they were two peas in a pod, and as youngsters, the adults enjoyed recalling their amusing shenanigans.

Aunt Marilyn came to the Home in a Greyhound bus on a cold

Saturday in mid-January. She lived 60 miles away and had entrusted her husband with the care of their two-year-old son and almost three-month-old daughter. Whenever Barb talked to me about Marilyn, she praised her for the supreme sacrifice her generous and sweet sister made for this brief visit! Barb recalled being so happy and relieved to see her, a familiar face who knew her people and understood her story. According to Barb, they held each other in a long embrace at the door. After discarding her coat, Aunt Marilyn took a handful of hard candy out of her pocketbook and handed them to Barb to take upstairs to enjoy after the visit. Since that meant climbing three flights of stairs to the full-length dormitory-type bedroom, Barb stuffed them into her coat pocket instead. She would have preferred cigarettes, but they weren't permitted in the Home.

Barb led her sister to the far corner of the living room, near the piano, which was the most private area in the room. I imagine theirs was a non-stop conversation about family and babies. They may have discussed deliveries since Aunt Marilyn had recently given birth to her daughter, Cathy. I didn't ask, and she didn't share the details of their conversation. Within the hour, they were getting bundled up and walking the outdoor path around the property to enjoy a bit more privacy. Barb said the time flew by, and before she knew it, she was giving her sister a long goodbye hug. She held back the tears until she could no longer see Marilyn, who boarded the Greyhound bus on North Hague Ave. to head back home.

Barb memorized her sister's last words: "It will all be over soon, Sis!" That was just like Marilyn, always positive and kind. They were "thick as thieves" as youngsters, and her encouragement aided her through many difficult situations over the years. According to my birth mom, this may have been the most challenging.

The other highlight was her outings beyond the premises. Twice a month, a trip to town in a station wagon was offered to each resident in the Home. Since the number of women and girls could fluctuate, not everyone went at the same time or in the same week. The mothers-to-be were driven to the local drugstore, and a staff person went inside to purchase the personal items they'd requested, using money they'd been given from their families.

Usually, the items consisted of candy, chewing gum, or toothpaste. Ahead of time, they were informed what could and could not be purchased with these funds. The girls remained in the vehicle the entire time. Barb said it was good to get away from the monotony of the regular chores. However, it was during those outings that she thought about her freedom as she watched people walking on the sidewalk beside the vehicle. She longed to return to her family.

Back at the Home, she spent her free time outdoors, walking around the vast premises. She began in the circular driveway with the other girls whose chores had been completed. Next, they went to the bridge near the entrance of the home and proceeded down the walkway that led to the vegetable and flower gardens. This provided them an opportunity to talk with one another and be out of the staff's earshot. They vented their frustrations and shared their fears during this time. She never mentioned whether they discussed their hopes for the future. Perhaps that seemed too far away while they were pregnant.

*

The trifold and my adoption documentation remained relatively untouched for the next ten years. That time was filled with endings and beginnings. We said goodbye to my childhood house and our hometown, and hello to retirement and adventures awaiting us in our new state. We enjoyed hours on our pontoon on Lake Cumberland, and I gained a passion for hiking in southern Kentucky and northern Tennessee. We took lots of trips and I wrote about each one of them.

However, the adoption box was never completely forgotten. As we became acquainted with neighbors and friends, a few heard the nudge stories and their curiosity aroused mine. I thought about Mom and wondered about her time in the Home. I tried to remember the contents of the trifold without going up into the attic and pulling it out of the container.

I hardly ever journaled in our cabin on the creek. I think I was worn out from all of the goodbyes. Instead, I wrote more letters to family back home, and added stories to my grandson's book of Jacob expressions. He spent a week with us each summer, and I recorded our fun-filled experiences after he returned home.

It wasn't until our last year in Somerset, Kentucky, that the urge to revisit the contents of my adoption container emerged. Ten years had come and gone since I'd experienced that unsettled feeling, but it was at the doorstep of my mind once again.

I'd spent the day hiking with friends on the Scuttlehole Trail, in the Daniel Boone National Forest, near London, Kentucky. I was riding back home with my dear friend, whose dad was my dad's law partner in Lima. We enjoyed our car rides together because it gave us an opportunity to reminisce about our families and growing up in Lima. She knew my story, and we talked about it most of the way to the church, where my car was parked.

After we parted ways, my mind started spinning. The following day, all of my documentation from the adoption box were spread out on the dining room table, and my curiosity was reignited.

It felt like the right time to learn more about this Home. Did the Home still exist? Why was it called the Friends Rescue Home? Who was being rescued? Why did my mother consider it a place of judgment? I was ready to discover the answers.

—Chapter 9—
A Day In The Home - 33 Stairs

A daily regimen, as dictated by others, was foreign to my birth mother. Her days of carefree living were non-existent while residing in the Home's group setting. The days of work and play, on her terms, came to a screeching halt the moment she walked through its threshold.

My birth mother didn't mention much about the furnishings on the inside of the Home, only stories about some of her experiences. I discovered the rest while reading a plethora of 1950s FRH fundraising brochures and looking through old photos around the time she was there. I have added those details to her typical day.

Here's how Barb described a typical day:
The bell rang at 6:30 A. M. to tell us it was time to wake up. Each day, I'd take my turn in the bathroom, dress, and make up my bed. Several of the girls descended the stairs to the kitchen to assist the dietician in preparing breakfast. Another bell would let us know it was time for breakfast, which meant walking down three flights of stair steps to begin the day and be seated at a table with all the familiar faces from the day before. Only the matron, nurse, and dietician knew

if a new face was joining us around one of the three eight-person rectangular tables in the afternoon or evening. In the morning, there was no mysterious newcomer.

Several girls set the four tables. Three long rectangular wooden dining room tables, with eight wooden spindle-back chairs, were for us girls, and the one square four-person table was for the matron (superintendent), the LPN, registered nurse, and the housekeeper/laundress.

One rectangular table was placed in front of the fireplace, while the other two were parallel to a lovely bay window. Each table setting had a crisp, ironed cloth napkin, a plate, glass, and silverware that had been donated to the Home by friends and interested individuals and churches.

In the Spring and summer months, we were told the superintendent permitted several of the girls to meet with the ground superintendent (gardener) near the garden in the back and side yard. They'd cut just enough flowers to fit into the three crystal vases that adorned the tables for that day. There were no flowers on the table when I was there.

The dining room mantel held very little and the room itself was fairly simple. A check patterned carpet and white drapes were the main features. A small, framed photo of the founder, and a few other pictures were on the walls, but nothing particularly striking.

A prayer was offered after everyone sat down. Each of us opened a cloth napkin and placed it on her lap before breakfast began.

The age range of these girls was 14-35, although the majority were seventeen and eighteen. I was 21.

When breakfast was finished, the kitchen staff directed those in charge of cleaning up while the rest of us headed to the chapel in the living room. The matron led us in devotions, consisting of hymn singing, sharing portions of scripture, and prayer. We were told that in the 1920s, the girls were requested to learn Bible verses during the morning. The verses were repeated at the evening meal. That was not our experience. After devotions, each of us was busy with her assigned daily tasks, which included washing, ironing, cleaning, and cooking. My job was to sweep while another girl mopped the floors in the large dormitory on the third floor. We took turns. I was further along in my pregnancy than she, so I only mopped the first month I was there.

I referred to the dormitory - style bedroom as the barracks. The room stretched the full length of the house and held 18 twin beds and 18 chairs, which were positioned to the side of the bed, acting as a nightstand, as well as a place to sit while putting on shoes, etc.

I walked down to the basement to get my supplies and carried them up to the main floor and began the march back up three flights of stairs. It was exhausting, and my work hadn't even begun. My job required us to move each heavy metal twin bed to be sure the entire floor surface was properly cleaned. Thankfully, there were always two girls in charge of this task.

At one time, the Home could accommodate up to twenty-three girls and twelve babies. By the time I was there, only 18 beds remained for the girls.

The routine was the same each weekday. When I completed my task, I marched my mop and bucket, or broom, back down all those steps, and another girl took them from the main floor down the basement steps to clean them. Then, we would begin the obligatory walks around the grounds to keep fit. The huge front porch offered comfortable seating to rest afterward. I remember sitting there often, even when it was chilly outdoors.

Most of the time, the walks were enjoyable. Occasionally, a group of school-aged children walked by, got a glimpse of the group, and whistled or taunted us. It was easy for me to ignore but not so much for the younger, school-aged girls. There would be tears, and one of the older girls would come alongside to wrap an arm around their shoulders or waist to provide comfort.

After dinner, we were encouraged to socialize and enjoy the grounds until dark. In the living room, there were several donated board games and puzzles that were available during poor weather conditions. If there was a pianist in the group, she might become the evening's special entertainment. Since I was there during the holidays, there was a decorated Christmas tree in the living room. We gathered around the piano and sang Christmas carols several times during that season.

The Friends provided small, practical gifts for each of us on Christmas morning, thanks to the generosity of several church groups and some local individuals. During a normal week, Tuesday was the day when a local or traveling minister and, if he was married, his wife would have a prayer meeting in the evening. The gospel was presented, and we were invited to ask Jesus into our lives. At 9:00, we retired to the dormitory on the third floor.

Sunday School was conducted by different preachers, or teachers in the community on Sunday afternoons at 3:00. We met several ladies who told us they were part of the Highlands Friends Church, a Quaker church that supported the Home monetarily, as well as with donations of time and gifts.

My Visit to the Friends Rescue Home

Thirty-three stair steps. I counted them each time I was in the Home. I remembered the story of my mother's days of sweeping the dormitory and imagined how taxing it must have been for her to go up and down those stairs. To my knowledge, Barb never counted the three flights of stair steps. I'm still not sure why I did. I was not carrying the weight of a baby in my belly or the weight of the world on my shoulders like she was.

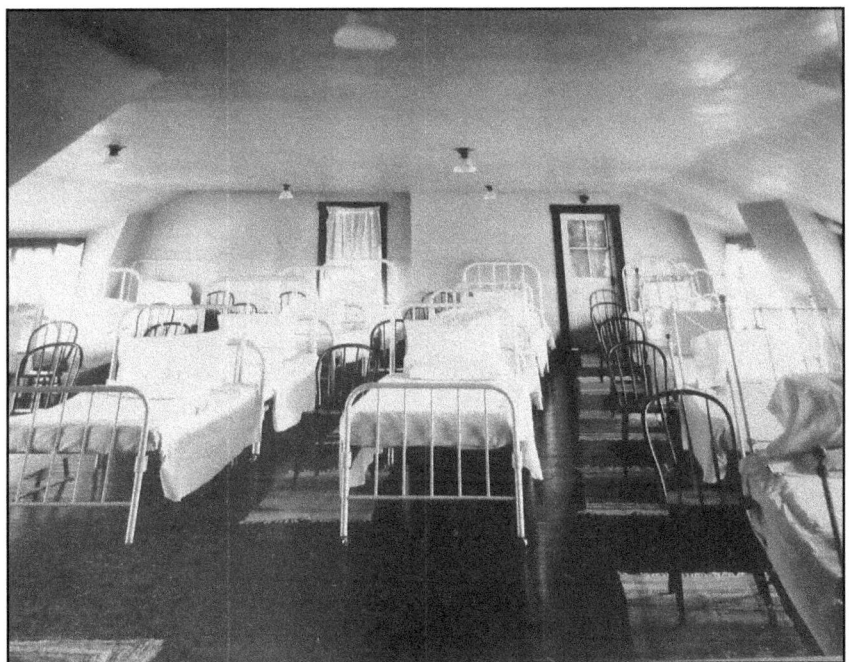

Ohio Yearly Meeting of Friends. (1933). The third-floor dormitory. [Photograph]. Friends Rescue Home annual fundraising brochure. (p. 3). (Photocopied with permission from the Archives Committee of Malone University and representatives from EFC-ER.)

Part II:
Other Family Members

—Chapter 10—
Barb's Dad and Mine

Barb's dad and mine had so much in common. Although my dad was 12 years younger than my biological granddad, both were actively involved in politics around the same time and in the same town. They had similar personalities, and although their political views were diametrically opposed, they cared about their community and invested a great deal of themselves in their attempts to improve it. Both spent hours in the county courthouse and dined in the same cafeteria frequently. It only stands to reason that the following conjectures are valid and entirely plausible.

The granddad I never knew was a loving father who embraced his daughter, my birth mother, in the midst of her crisis, and provided her with the ability to bring me into the world safely. By most accounts, he was a fine man. Called "Doc" because he operated a drug store downtown, his only "degree' was in public service, and he offered himself up to his community for 45 years.

My curiosity about my dad and granddad's relationship was heightened when I discovered their names and signatures on the same document. The year was 1956, two years after I was born. My dad had just been elected a member of the Republican County Central Committee from his precinct. As the director of the Board of Elections, my biological granddad's signature was one of several that appeared, verifying the accuracy of the election.

My dad and granddad, although they didn't know their connection at the time, frequently ate lunch in Jack's Cafeteria, the local downtown hub and eatery for judges, attorneys, and all those with political aspirations. The group gathered at a round table for lunch and discussed the pressing issues of the day. I'm told it could get very heated, but at the end of the conversation, warm handshakes were exchanged in spite of the differing opinions. Often, I wonder if this food establishment may have been where the initial adoption conversation commenced and a plan was conceived.

It's quite possible that Jack's Cafeteria played a significant role in securing my birth mother's place in an unwed mother's home just 90 miles away. In the months preceding my birth, my granddad was 46 years old and running for mayor of the city. My dad, at 34 years of age, was establishing his law practice after having served in the Korean Conflict. After twenty-nine-plus years of gathering information, I found a reliable source who verified that my adoptive dad told my mom that he knew my biological family. Earlier in my investigation, my biological aunt and uncle told me they remembered their dad frequenting Jack's often and that it wouldn't surprise them if that was where they met. In the 50s, my dad's law office was directly across the street from Jack's Cafeteria, and I recall him telling me he ate lunch there at least twice a week for years.

I can only imagine the confidential exchange that ensued, perhaps hours poring over where my birth mom might go. Having been raised in Delaware and Columbus, Ohio, my dad was very familiar with Columbus, so the unwed mother's home that was chosen seems logical, given his knowledge and ability to connect the dots. He was one who knew how to navigate through new information long before Google was discovered.

Some things I can only imagine, but what I do know is that while I was still in grade school, my dad came home from work one day with a beautiful, two-foot-tall bride doll. I remember squealing with delight as he handed her to me. I told him she was wonderful and thanked him profusely. This kind of elaborate gift-giving was rare in my household. Dolls were Christmas presents. Mom Lawson walked in with a less-than-delighted look on her face and asked where he had gotten her. He proceeded to tell her it was brought to his office by someone who had been in Marysville. That was all I heard, as I knew nothing about Marysville or anyone living there. My new, prized possession and I were on our way to my bedroom. I plopped down on my bed and began looking at this exquisite doll with her lovely layers of white fabric adorned with lace, chiffon, organza, and an underskirt of crinoline. Lace embellished the bodice, the bottom, and the neckline. Her veil covered the bodice of her gown. I had never seen such a grand doll. She had curly blonde hair and crystal blue eyes. She was so elegant compared to my Chatty Cathy.

I gently placed her in my child-sized black rocking chair so she would be the first thing I saw each morning. She was perfect. Less than a month later, she was gone. I asked my mother what had happened to her, and she said she and Dad had decided the gift was not appropriate, given the circumstances.

I asked why and who it was who had given her to me. She simply said that I would have to talk with my dad when he got home from work. As you can imagine, those were the first questions he heard when entering our house that evening. He told me that a young woman's parents wanted to thank him for helping their daughter through a difficult time in her life. They knew Dad had a young daughter, and this was the gift chosen. He and mom decided it was not an appropriate gift and they should not accept it. I was so disappointed, but my doll was gone, and that was that. I just assumed the lovely doll was given back to her. When I was a teenager, my dad told me more about the young woman and the doll. She had been incarcerated at the Ohio Reformatory for Women in Marysville, Ohio. Dad was her legal representative, and it was a pro bono case. So as not to upset the gift giver, Dad took the doll to an agency that gave out dolls and toys to underprivileged children at Christmastime.

Was there a connection between the reformatory and the rescue home where Barb stayed? Perhaps. I was unable to directly connect the Friends Rescue Home with the Reformatory, but wondered if there was an invisible "string" that connected them to the family who wanted to thank my dad for his work on their daughter's behalf.

In my research, I learned that in 1911 a separate women's penal institution was authorized by the Ohio General Assembly.

On June 25, 1914, Evangeline Reams, founder of the Friends Rescue Home, had a mission that stretched beyond the grounds of the Home to that very same area where the Ohio Reformatory for Women operates to this day, near Marysville, Ohio. Evangeline had gone to this community and presented her vision, as documented in a Marysville Journal Tribune article. Miss Reams made the trip to Marysville, Ohio, 30 miles away from the Home, to explain the need for funding the Friends Rescue Home since it had become a Protestant nondenominational home. Two years later, in 1916, Evangeline became the Superintendent of Gilead Social Training School for Delinquent Women, located in East Columbus. On September 1, 1916, the Ohio Department of Rehabilitation and Corrections opened The Ohio Reformatory for Women in Marysville. This was less than forty miles from the Home.

I wonder if Evangeline's meeting that day had any bearing on the reformatory placement in Marysville, Ohio.

Perhaps there is no connection at all beyond the fact that two acquaintances, my dad and granddad, came together with a plan that benefited both of their beloved daughters.

—Chapter 11—
The Connection Nudge

I wish I could go back in time and peer into the mind of my adoptive dad in 1953. Did he have a God nudge before discussing adopting a child with his wife, who could not conceive, and their doctor, who favored the idea of adoption? Or was it after he learned of my birth mother's pregnancy from my granddad or someone else? After all, my granddad was very good friends with several attorneys in town, and one of them was even a godfather to Barb's younger sister, Shirley. How was Dad able to compartmentalize his life in order to keep the secret safe in our small town after I was born? He was always very good at keeping a secret. Perhaps that came from years of complete submission to the client-attorney confidentiality pledge he vowed to uphold in his law practice.

As an adopted child in the 50s, I learned to compartmentalize my own life at a young age. Adoption discussion was off the table of appropriate topics in our home because it was private, and privacy was to be respected, so it was "stored" in an imaginary box labeled "adoption."

There were other boxes, but not as significant as this one. The adoption box was easy to keep on the shelf unless I told a friend.

However, my dad would have had to bump into my biological granddad from time to time. As a practicing attorney, Dad frequented the Law library that was housed in the Allen County courthouse where my granddad's office was after he was elected chairman of the Allen County Board of Elections in 1955, the year after I was born. As the years went by, were there ever whispers exchanged about me when they met? Did God ever nudge Dad into sharing anything about me, or did they leave that particular part of their lives, that box, at the door of Jack's Cafeteria as they entered to "chew the fat" with the other lawyers and politicians of their day? I'll never know. They are both deceased, and those secrets are safe forever.

However, some secrets have been unearthed in my research over the years.

One such secret came to light from a God nudge. For as long as I can recall, my parents were actively involved in leadership roles in the church where we worshiped. Dad became very good friends with a gentleman in the same Presbytery whose family attended a church 30 miles away. They hit it off immediately, and before long, they introduced their wives, and the four of them began to enjoy an occasional evening out.

It was not long after those evenings together that their daughter, Becky, and I were introduced, and our friendship began. We spent time together at each other's houses in the summertime and planned our week at Camp Premauca, a Presbyterian church camp in Michigan, based on each other's schedules. One year, Becky's mom convinced my mom to be a camp counselor during the week that we were there. Mom Lawson had been a Girl Scout leader but had only once agreed to be a camp counselor, thanks to the prodding of Becky's mom. Our families stayed in touch for years but got together less frequently after Becky and I were adults.

Decades later, Becky and I became Facebook friends, in spite of the fact that we had not seen one another or spoken over the phone for over 45 years. Several years after we reconnected, Becky's only child died from a sudden heart attack. After learning of this tragedy from Facebook posts, I sent her a message conveying my deepest sympathy regarding this tragedy. I thought about calling her, but it just didn't feel right since we had lost touch all those years ago.

So, I sent cards to her instead. During the following year, she shared her grief through her comments and those of her friends on Facebook. Occasionally, I sent her a private message, asking how she and her husband were doing. We truly got reacquainted during that year. The day before the first anniversary of her child's passing, I began experiencing that unsettling feeling I had become accustomed to, which I identified as a God nudge. All I could think about was Becky, her husband, and the sorrow they must be feeling.

At first, I thought it unwise to call her. I hadn't reached out to her, except in private messages, the entire year. What comfort would I be to her now? I struggled all morning to make sense of it and finally succumbed to the nudge and called. As our conversation unfolded, it was as if time had not elapsed since our last chat as young women. I told her the reason for my call, and within minutes, the tears flowed as she shared stories about her wonderful son.

Fifteen minutes into our conversation, she changed the subject. I'll never forget the timeframe because I looked at my computer to see the exact time. She asked me if I thought that my musical talent came from my biological parents or if it was environmental in nature since everyone in my adoptive family played an instrument in their youth. At that moment, I understood what the term "shell-shocked" meant. I couldn't speak -- completely caught off guard. I asked how in the world she knew I was adopted. I had never told her. She proceeded to tell me a story about our mothers during that week of church camp when we were youngsters. One evening, Mom and Lois were alone, talking about everything under the sun, or stars in this case. Out of nowhere, Mom told Lois that I was adopted. As she shared some of the details, she told Lois that my dad had offered to tell her about my biological family since he knew them. Mom said she refused to hear the information because she never wanted to lie to me if I ever asked her. If she didn't know, she wouldn't have anything to tell me. I don't know why she thought she would have had to lie. Perhaps she didn't want me to have the information, and this was her way of protecting herself in any future conversation.

I would never have known about this had I not acted on that

nudge to contact Becky.

Several months later, I had a conversation with Lois, who was then in her 90s. She repeated that entire story to me about the conversation with my adopted mother. Sadly, she passed away just a few months later. The nudge was perfectly timed. I have come to believe it always is. My nudge to provide a bit of comfort to my friend also added more pieces to my adoption puzzle!

To date, the most life-changing nudge was the one guiding me to my birth mom. However, each nudge has contributed to the significant bridge to connect the past to my present.

—Chapter 12—

Barb's Girls

Barb's second daughter, my sister Linda, has become one of my dearest friends. As in all deep and lasting relationships, it has taken time to nurture it.

From the moment I met my mother, I knew she was mine. Looking into her eyes, I saw my eyes reflecting back to me. During our first meeting, Barb told me she knew I was hers because I reminded her so much of my sister Linda. The three of us had that undeniable biological connection from the very beginning.

When we're together, my sister and I are asked whether we are twins almost as often as whether we are sisters. The similarities in appearance are uncanny. Although Irish twins are defined as siblings born less than 12 months apart, siblings eighteen months or less are often considered Irish twins, as well. Linda is eighteen months younger, and we're Irish! Whatever one chooses to call it, we have become very close to one another.

What has been remarkable is how similar our tastes are since we weren't raised together. Years before we met, we had the same hairstyle, dressed alike, and even wore the same sweater in one of our "teacher" pictures at our schools. Both of us enjoy photography and traveling to new places. We are passionate about our families and the sacred space they hold in our lives.

During conversations, we've learned of the many connections tying us together over the years. One of my best grade school friends became one of Linda's best friends in high school. As a cellist in the high school orchestra, I became friends with another one of Linda's best friends, who played the harp and sat near me during high school practices and performances. She lived directly behind me in the next block.

For a year, Linda and I attended the same junior high school together. She was in 7th grade, and I was in 8th. When I was a 6th grader, our school sustained a massive fire, destroying 31 classrooms and the cafeteria area. We were sent to a nearby church annex and Franklin Elementary School, which was behind the original junior high school, from March until the end of my 8th-grade year.

Two new middle schools were constructed the following year, and Linda and I didn't attend the same one. Both of us would attend the same high school for one year. Our high school was composed of 10th, 11th, and 12th-grade students. When Linda was a sophomore and I was a junior, she lived in Jamaica with our mom and her new husband. They came back in March of that year, and she completed her sophomore year in Lima. We walked the same high school hallways from March of 1971 until June of the following year without meeting one another or realizing we were full sisters.

In the early 1970s, we lived right around the corner from one another, only two and one-half short blocks away. A mere eight houses separated us, and we never knew it.

Linda and I appeared in our high school yearbook in the same photo for the Block L club, a girls' cheering section for boys' basketball games, which was common in those days. In this picture, we are two rows and three girls from one another. Incredible! That particular year, our paths of study in high school were different. She was in the secretarial block, and I was college-bound. As a senior, I was actively involved in organizations and senior activities, as well as a job and a boyfriend.

Additionally, our family had invited an exchange student, Veronica

Lee Duarte, into our home for the year. Vicky was from Guatemala, and we were the same age and both seniors in high school. She was in the secretarial block, but when I asked her if she knew Linda, she didn't recall meeting or seeing her.

After high school, I attended the University of Kentucky for two years. I came home, married my high school sweetheart in 1974, became the Teen Director at the YWCA, and continued to attend classes in the evening at the Ohio State University branch campus in Lima. At the end of her junior year in high school, Linda decided she was college-bound, too. She attended her freshman year of college at the OSU branch campus in our hometown and then moved to the main campus to complete her degree.

She came back home in the summers to work and attend a few classes. I took classes at the Lima campus, too, but they were held during different quarters. By the time she was taking classes there, I was taking classes at another college in the area: Bluffton College. Both of us worked in the schools. She became a middle school reading teacher, and I became a paraprofessional in a Severely Behaviorally Handicapped classroom, as it was called then, before finishing my career in charge of our county's Alternative High School short-term classroom.

Similar interests surfaced as we got to know one another. We both enjoy reading – she, perhaps more than me. We love animals – I, perhaps more than she. One year, we gave each other the same book for Christmas. It still amazes us that we also sent out the exact Christmas card that year. We love the same Christmas movie, "White Christmas," and have enjoyed the tradition of watching it together during several of our annual sister Christmas gatherings.

Although we were raised in different family situations, we had one phenomenal and analogous ingredient in common: the unconditional love of our family. The mothers who raised us had some similar traits. Although Mom Lawson was a stay-at-home mother and Barb was the breadwinner of their family of two, both provided for our needs but, perhaps from a certain distance sometimes.

My dad was only present on the weekends. He filled his evenings with civic organization obligations that my parents thought were necessary for his career, as well as the community. Kenny, the man Linda called "Dad," entered her life when she was a teenager. From Barb and Linda's descriptions, he was a great man, and a wonderful father figure for Linda. I'm thankful Kenny and Barb enjoyed twenty-two years of marriage together.

Our DNA explains our similar physical and perhaps our mental make-up, just as our being single–or relatively single–children accounts for some of our emotional similarities. It would appear that we often saw ourselves through a similar lens filter.

We continue to enjoy many holidays and special occasions together. Most siblings have occasional issues, and we're no different. It has been my experience that adoptees reunited with their siblings have a complex set of roadblocks to negotiate if they want their relationship to last. The same could be said of their siblings.

Linda and I consider our time together sacred and essential. To commemorate the thirtieth anniversary of our first meeting, we hiked up Mt. Le Conte in the Smoky Mountains. We have been on many other trips and hiking adventures together over the years. We are convinced that our moments together continue to elevate our love for one another. Each time provides us another opportunity to peer into the windows of each other's pasts and pull out a memory not previously shared, thereby making our understanding of one another richer.

I like to remember a day when Barb, Linda, and I were in a department store together. Mom had gotten tired of our dawdling over which checkered cloth napkins to purchase and walked on to find another item. However, she took a moment to turn around and look at us. Later, she remarked that it was as if our two heads were one. Then, she smiled. I would like to think that some of her most peaceful moments were those in which the three of us were together, enjoying one another's company. Privately, she may have had moments of sadness knowing we were not together in our youth. But then, she would move on, as she always did. In adulthood, our path to one another has been of benefit to all three of us.

I always wanted a sister while I was growing up. I'm so thankful that Linda is mine.

—Chapter 13—

My Grandparents

I never met my maternal adoptive grandmother, as she and her husband passed many years before I was born. I heard stories and have a few black and white photos narrating their lives, but unfortunately, that is all that remains.

My paternal, adoptive grandma was the one I knew in my youth, and like her only son, I felt unconditionally loved by her. She was the typical grandma of the 50s and 60s. Her long silver hair, parted down the middle of her head, was always softly coiffed in a bun at the back of her head. She wore "Grandma shoes" which were laced up and low-heeled. A long-pleated print dress was her daily attire, and I rarely saw her without her well-worn apron wrapped around her girth. She had beautiful piercing blue eyes, an Aignes-Hopewood trait, and was stern and well respected. From my perspective, she definitely "wore the pants" in the family.

As a youngster it felt like my grandparents lived far away. In reality, it was a two-hour drive from door to door. In the late 50s and early 60s, we didn't travel like we do today. Therefore, our time together was during family holiday gatherings at Thanksgiving and every Christmas, my week with them in the summer, and Saturday pregame lunches before heading to the local college football games with my parents. She was quite the reader and a good seamstress. She would shower me with paperback books, and taught me how to care for a flower garden and cocker spaniels.

One of my favorite memories of her will always be watching her present dinner around their large wooden dining room table that seemed to take up most of the dining room. As I recall, there was always a tablecloth, and the China setting seemed fancy to me. Large meals were prepared in a less than adequate kitchen with little ventilation. Her small kitchen was always messy, but she knew her way around it. Braunschweiger on rye, or pumpernickel bread, with Swiss cheese, was on our lunch plate if we were preparing to head to a football game.

For a treat, during my week with her in the summer, I would look forward to a peanut butter and raisin sandwich or a vanilla ice cream cone with raisins in the bottom of the cone, in between scoops, and on top of it. Until recently, I gave Grandma Lawson the credit for the raisin-filled delicacies. I thought she was convinced raisins were an essential daily food requirement. Alas, Grandpa Lawson was the inventor, and he added raisins to ice cream cones like I add chocolate chips to my grandchildren's homemade cookies.

Meals were the only times I recall Grandma sitting down for any length of time. I think she counted on my younger cousin, Winni, to be my entertainment for the week, and she was correct. To my knowledge, there was only one time that she regretted that decision.

We had been dropped off at the city swimming pool for the day. At that time, there was no sunscreen and, unlike my cousin who was used to being in the sun all day long, I was not. So, I became burnt to a crisp. Back at my grandmother's, I lay flat on the bed where my dad and two aunts had been born, which at the time seemed creepy. I wore only underpants and Grandma doused my body frequently with witch hazel, while sitting beside the bed and shaking her head. I remember feeling sorry for her, although I was the one in physical pain. I could sense her emotional anguish at having misjudged the outcome of a "fun" day at the pool.

My mom and her mother-in-law shared a love of sewing. Frequently, their conversation revolved around their current projects. Grandma Lawson embroidered a sweet bunny design on a baby blanket that she presented to me after I was born. She embellished it with appliques and I treasure it.

I have always admired those who lovingly labor for hours over the cutting, piecing together, binding, and hand stitching of their one-of-a-kind quilt. Masterpieces, every one of them. By far the most special to me is my grandmother's blue and white Lone Star patterned quilt topper. It has eight diamond-shaped pieces in each block that meet in the center. Surrounding the diamonds are sixteen triangles. If the angles of the diamonds are off by even a fraction, or the pieces are not assembled accurately, the quilt top will curl or buckle when it's stitched and no amount of pulling or tugging will correct the problem.

Grandma's was by no means perfect, but nonetheless lovely. She created it in the 1940s probably out of my grandpa's old work shirts, well-worn church shirts, as well as some purchased material. It is beautiful to me because her hands worked the material and bound each piece together meticulously. Although incomplete, it's my opinion that she completed the most important part of the quilt. One may spend countless hours actually quilting the pieces together but, if your topper is not beautiful, all is in vain.

I'm convinced it had special meaning to her, but I was never privy to the details. The topper started after my brother's birth in 1944. Perhaps, it was meant to be his. I imagine her cutting and piecing it together while drifting into thoughts of her first grandchild and all that would lie ahead. She would soon invite her son, daughter-in-law and young grandson to live with them in their converted bedroom in their attic while her son, my dad, finished law school. Maybe the quilt brought her pleasure, having something to occupy her hands in her living room, after she had completed her daily tasks and was listening to the sounds of her loved ones above her.

I continue to wonder why she never completed it. Grandma had finished three quilts, two for her daughters when they were born and a red and white one for my dad. She completed slipcovers, drapes, aprons, smocks, and dresses. She would set up her Singer on the dining room table and whirl away using the foot control which she had positioned on the table. The extreme pain in her varicose-veined legs caused her to use her hand on the control instead of her foot.

I wonder if her life took a turn and her time was spent elsewhere, or if it simply took too long to complete the blue and white Lone Star topper, so she chose to let it go for the time being.

My heart has always been drawn to it, a reminder of things left incomplete and yet, still lovely and useful. I tend to think we are all in this state until our passing. Incomplete until our final breaths. It is also a thoughtful reminder that conversations about life experiences are valuable and should be passed on to those we love. I choose to keep it in my view as a reminder of my grandma and the brevity of life.

The topper has had many homes, as have we. For years, it took up residence with my other quilts in a large wicker basket. The Lone Star topper would begin at the top and eventually end up at the bottom of the basket as others were preferred for their warmth. One day, I carefully lifted it out and gently placed it over the back of my favorite rocker and there it rested until we moved from Ohio to Michigan. Many books were read while I leaned against it. The topper faded and became tattered from the direct sunlight and the occasional laundering. That didn't matter.

A few years later, it was displayed on a ceiling shelf among old lanterns, driftwood, and wooden shorebirds at our lake house. Several friends commented on its uniqueness and were surprised to learn it was not a completed piece. It laid at the end of our guest bed in our cabin on the creek when we first moved to Kentucky. It didn't match anything in the room, but it brought me pleasure to see it there, as well as to place it on the bed after freshening the linens when a guest left. In my opinion, it is currently in its best surroundings. It covers my granddaughters' dollhouse and each time it is uncovered, which is often, the mysterious story of their great-great grandmother's quilt topper and her labor of love is recited in hopes that it continues to have value to the next generation. Beloved and incompletely perfect.

My grandparents lived a very simple, midwestern lifestyle. I didn't see much of my grandpa during the summer weeks I visited them. He became a bus driver in 1933, when Columbus changed to trolley coaches due to the Great Depression, and many streetcar lines were closed in North America. During the streetcar era, Columbus had been given the nickname "Arch City."

In 1911, the wooden arches used to light the city with gas lamps were replaced by metal arches and powered by electric light bulbs. These arches also carried the power lines for a recently electrified streetcar system. At the beginning of World War II, some of the streetcar lines were used by civilians commuting to war related factory jobs during the time when gasoline and rubber tires were rationed. But by 1965, the trolley coaches were no longer used, so my grandpa became a diesel bus driver which afforded him the opportunity to trade coins as he added up his earnings for the day.

He began what would become a stellar collection of unusual coins, a hobby he passed down to his only son. My dad added to Grandpa's collection by bringing home coins while stationed in different countries during his military service in WWII and the Korean War. Grandpa was very proud of his collection. He was a quiet man who told a story with his eyes. He would smirk at the end, and no matter if I understood the humor or not, his countenance made me smile. What remains with me is the smell of the cherry tobacco he smoked in his favorite pipe.

Thanks to my initial nudge from God, I was blessed with eleven wonderful years with my maternal grandma, the only biological grandmother I will ever know. She was Barb's mother and she was precious to me. As with my birth mother and sister, I felt a strong connection immediately, and my life has much more continuity thanks to our years together.

Both of us possessed a love for the written word, in journal writing and poetry composition. We enjoyed playing cards, watching football, and traveling. She could be very funny, and she was quite spunky in a quiet way. My favorite memories of her are listening to her stories at Mom's kitchen island. While watching a few OSU football games together, I began to understand where my strong competitive instincts originated.

Another precious memory was that of taking my five-year-old

daughter to her great-grandmother's house at Christmastime. I will always remember the serene look on both of their faces as my sweet daughter learned how to make the very best tasting popcorn balls from her adored great-grandma. It was one of my grandma's favorite treats, and the family could wrap many memories around watching her make caramel popcorn or caramel popcorn balls, and place them in the designated pan for everyone to enjoy.

On this occasion, I did not participate in the instruction, preparation or the creation. Rather, I was delighted to take my front row seat to this very special interaction; that of two generations finding pleasure in one another's company while participating in a fun activity that brought them closer. To this day, if I close my eyes, I can see the room, smell the caramel popcorn balls, hear my grandma's voice reminding Hilly to be careful handling the hot caramel while forming the balls, see their smiles and hear the giggles as Grandma told her stories, and experience, once again, the warm feeling that consumed me while witnessing this simple, but grand exchange on a winter afternoon.

GRANDMAS - PART 2
WHEN IT HURTS TO BE ADOPTED

Barb would never know about the tug of emotional turmoil I occasionally experienced. I chose to withhold it from her. She had dealt with enough of that in her lifetime. Our moments together were spent enjoying the bond we had established and the irreplaceable memories we gathered.

I am fond of a recent photo I took in our hometown cemetery. My sister and I are standing, like bookends, with our great-great-grandparents' family monument in between us, and surrounded by the graves of our other ancestors wrapped around us in the shape of a rectangle. In reflecting upon the process of taking the image, in addition to the picture itself, I came up with an analogy of how the lives of my sister and I fit into our family. My sister always knew who she was and whose she was. She was firmly planted in the picture waiting for me to set the timer and run to my spot. Linda was always present while I had to find my "space" or place in the frame of the lens or, in this instance, within the family. After almost 30 years, there are still times when I am attempting to find my space.

I'm fortunate that I've only had a few experiences dealing with emotional turmoil while attempting to find that space meant only for me. I choose to believe most were unintentional, but they hurt, nonetheless. One example was the day my biological grandmother passed. She had been hospitalized and was in deteriorating health. I visited with her several days earlier and was aware of her frail condition. On Sunday morning, I decided to go up to her hospital room for a quick visit before heading to church for the morning service at 11:00 AM. I arrived in her room at 10:15, and she was not there. Immediately, I inquired at the nurses' station and was politely asked who I was. I told them I was her granddaughter, and one of the nurses came from behind the station, held my elbow and softly told me that she had passed at 5:05 AM. I was stunned. She was 92 years old but I was not prepared for that news. The nurse asked if I needed to sit down and I said "no" and that I needed to leave for church.

My eyes filled with tears, but the weeping didn't commence until I was safely tucked away from sight behind the wheel of my car in the parking lot. I was overwhelmed in a way I had never experienced. I was really sad. Just so sad. Years later, I remember wondering why no one had called me. I wasn't angry, but sad and hurt. *Did I fit in the periphery of this family or perhaps, not at all?* I had been a part of my biological family's life for over eleven years. I had been with several family members when I visited Grandma in the hospital, and several of them had my phone number. I chose not to expose my disappointment, but rather to believe that it was an honest mistake, as her loss was a devastating time for everyone who loved her.

In contrast, the comment made in my adoptive grandmother's home, after she and my grandfather passed, was definitely not a mistake. My dad was the executor of their estate. He had two sisters, one brother-in-law, and two nieces. With my mom, brother and me, that made nine of us, excluding spouses and grandchildren. Small family. It should have been a simple process.

Dad decided we should all be present at my grandparent's house at 10:00 AM. As a group, we were advised that we would methodically go through the house together, room by room, and everyone could pick out what they would like to keep. When we were done making our choices, there'd be an auction to sell the remainder of the household items. The money taken in from the auction would be distributed equally between the three siblings.

As often happens, it didn't go as planned. One sister decided she was entitled to most of the valuables in the house. It was upstairs, in one of the two guest bedrooms, that the conversation occurred. The discussion revolved around who should have the bed where my dad and his sisters had been born. It was part of my grandparent's first bedroom suite, dark maple and in relatively good condition, considering its age.

I expressed an interest. My aunt ignored my comment and proceeded to announce that it should stay in the Lawson family. That was one of the few times I felt like I was *out* of the Lawson family picture frame completely. Neither of my parents responded to her comment. Shortly afterward, my mom said she would take it. We never spoke of it again, but when my parents passed, my brother asked me to take it if I still wanted it. He had remembered, and this touched my heart. I think my mom knew that is where it would end up. She just chose not to make it an issue that day.

There was only one other thing that I wanted from that house. It was Grandma's old rocking chair that had been sitting on her front porch for years. I remember watching her rock in that chair as my cousin and I played outdoors when I went for my annual summer visit. But, alas, that same aunt told me she wanted it on her front porch.

Again, the angst. I have always believed God gave me a composed, slow to anger temper on purpose. My tendency is to get angry long after the incident that evoked the emotion. Usually, I forget the words someone says but not the intent. I believe hers was a statement as to my place, or lack of place, in the family.

As an adult, I wondered what led my aunt to make that comment. After having begun this journey, I have become keenly aware of the simple fact that by not knowing a person's past, it is almost impossible to completely understand their reasoning in the present. I do not know what pain she suffered from others, and I know the only part I have in her story is one of forgiveness. I've not walked in her shoes and in so many ways, she was kind to me. I will choose to leave it at that.

Our lives are like a vapor or "a mist that appears for a little while and then vanishes" (James 4:14 NIV) and the things that we obtain in this life will not hold a candle to the relationships we have chosen to devote our time and our hearts to cultivate. I know that both of my families have loved me, and they have shown me, over and over again, that family is complicated, complex and one of the best spaces in which to reside. That is, if you are willing to be jostled around from time to time. I'm willing.

—Chapter 14—
She Lingers

Barb loved being the life of the party. She could light up a room just by walking into it. When she told a joke, the twinkle in her eyes caused a smile to sweep across the faces of those in her presence long before the punchline was even uttered. Sadly, she left the room too soon, but her spirit lingers long after the laughter has faded.

My Mom, Barb, passed peacefully on December 30th, 2009, just two years after my adoptive mother was laid to rest and three years after my adoptive dad. Mom had chosen not to undergo tests for a predictable lung cancer diagnosis. She had smoked the majority of her life, and her deteriorating lung capacity and difficulty breathing were the telltale signs. She had been hospitalized Christmas night for these issues. Many in the family were able to visit with her over the weekend. My sister, Linda, spent a night in her hospital room and told us Mom had been extremely uncomfortable and restless. It was obvious she was in excruciating pain.

Early Tuesday morning, my aunt was given the doctor's report on Mom's condition and suggestions for her care. She wrote it down on a tablet beside Mom's bed so that we would see it when we arrived. The attending physician said her pneumonia was serious. He noted that her breathing was difficult and labored. The pulmonologist came in shortly after the attending physician left and added that he wanted to see her in one month to do a lung biopsy, since he believed her condition to be lung cancer. He thought she needed to go to a nursing home to get 24-hour daycare for at least two weeks, possibly longer. He recommended that she talk with a Social Worker to discuss arrangements, but Mom refused. She told him she just wanted to go home and that she had a daughter to take care of her. Again, the doctor strongly suggested a nursing home so that they could monitor her as she had two kinds of bacterial infections and needed antibiotics through an IV.

When she refused a second time, he recommended that she stay in the hospital for at least two more days and reconsider her nursing home option. Her mind was made up, and she wanted no more tests, probing or discussions about a nursing facility for rehabilitation. She was in too much pain and misery, mentally and physically. She chose palliative care.

Her two sisters, Linda and I spent most of that day with her. I stayed behind when my aunts and sister departed that afternoon. Later when I reached the door to leave, Mom asked me if I thought she had made the right decision, and if it would be ok with God. I was at a loss for words. I walked back in the room and put her hand in both of mine for what seemed like a long time. I told her that I loved her very much and that I had no answers. I said that I could see how miserable she was and how much she was hurting. If she didn't want to go through all the tests and procedures, it was her right to refuse. Only God knew what was best for her, and I promised to continue to pray for her to sense His peace, whatever her decision.

That evening, I went back to the hospital to spend the night with her. It was the hospital's policy to move a patient in palliative care to a different floor. When I arrived, Mom was asleep in her new room. The medication that was administered allowed her to rest very peacefully. She continued to sleep and sadly, I would never see her gorgeous, celadon green eyes again.

That evening I told her everything I was feeling about our years together. Since she was in palliative care and heavily sedated due to the pain she was experiencing, she was unable to respond. I was thankful she wasn't suffering. She was there and with her was the only place I wanted to be. We had enjoyed many lively conversations over those seventeen years of getting to know one another. As much as I yearned for more time with her, I was resolved to creating a peaceful, calm environment until she took her last breath.

That night I laughed and cried as I reminisced. Then, in the wee hours of the morning, I read to her from my Bible, verses that were meaningful to me and brought me peace. Later, I held her hand as I drifted off to sleep in the chair beside her bed. The night went by quickly, and my three hours of sleep must have been deep, because I felt very rested in the morning when the family began to arrive.

Her final day was quiet, which was not in keeping with her large personality and zest for fun. God chose for her to linger all day and into the evening before she passed away that night. It was a blue moon. How appropriate. She lingered long enough for everyone who wanted to come and see her. Several friends arrived throughout the evening. Some stayed while others came to offer a heartfelt hug or a kind word, then left quietly.

To me, the most touching demonstration of love was from my son who lived two hours away. He arrived after work that evening. He walked up to the nurse's station and asked the nurse on duty to tell me he was there, and ask if it was a convenient time for me to come away from his grandmother's bedside. My sister and I walked out to him and our husbands followed behind. I'll not forget his tender voice as he hugged me.

"I'm really sorry, Mom. I know she was special to you."

Seventeen years earlier his maternal great-grandmother had prayed for him when he'd been involved in a life-threatening car accident, not knowing he was related to her. She died six years earlier, and now her daughter was at death's door. He chose to be present and offer comfort to me. He had only been in his biological grandmother's presence a few times, but he knew how I felt about her. It was a precious blessing in the midst of my deep sadness.

Sweet memories were shared by those wrapped around Barb's hospital bed and others seated in chairs. Laughter and tears flooded the room, over and over again that evening.

Mom loved to make others laugh and she loved to laugh, but that night there were more tears than laughter. Her light was extinguishing, and we were grieving her loss before her last breath was taken. The hope she had of heaven and seeing the Jesus she had come to love gave us pause to smile. By the time I met her, she was well versed in her beliefs and her choice to move forward without looking over her shoulder at the past and the choices she made as a young woman. She was at peace that our lives had reunited and could easily talk to me about her life, before, during and after my adoption.

"No regrets," she would say. "I thought I had no other choice at the time and looking back, I really didn't!" She would tell me how grateful she was that I had been placed into a good family who loved me. Once she told me that knowing that fact was not only a relief to her but brought her happiness, as did our reunion in 1992.

Within the hour that she passed, her youngest sister began reciting the "Lord's Prayer" and the rest of us joined her. One could have heard a pin drop in the moments after the last word was spoken. "AMEN" --may it be so in accordance with Your will.

When she passed, the world did not stand still. For months following that evening I was sad. However, in time, I felt an unusual peace. I don't believe that our passing is an ending. It's merely a passage because our souls continue. What had changed, and what was new to me, was that Barb's life was in mine now forever. She had always been an essential part of me, even before I knew her name or could identify her in a photo. I hadn't felt the same attachment when my adoptive parents passed just a few years earlier! Our stories aligned, and I loved them dearly. I was heartbroken after burying them. Many of the things I learned before their passing stuck with me and I find myself saying what they would have said in different situations. But the biological connection lives on in those we leave behind. Their lives are in ours, and ours will be in those who live on when we no longer walk this earth. This thought brought me such peace.

I chose not to be added to my mother's newspaper obituary. It was kind of my sister to ask. I was honored to have added some information to her obituary and that was enough. Most of her family knew about me, but some did not. Some of her closest friends knew, but many did not. The obituary was to celebrate her life. No surprises were appropriate. Additionally, my adoptive brother, Walt, had just received a cancer diagnosis that month. I wasn't sure if my parents had informed him about the discovery of my birth mother since he wasn't living in Lima at the time. Now was not a good time to "connect the dots." He passed away far too soon –exactly five years later.

The day after she passed, Mom's visitation and funeral were planned. As the executrix, my sister was in charge of all the details regarding Mom's will. Later in the day I joined my sister and niece at Mom's house and went through photos that were added to poster boards for the visitation. A slight scent of Claire Burke's Christmas Memories Holiday Room Spray greeted me at the door and wafted through each room of the house. It was her favorite scent during the holidays.

After consulting my sister and receiving her approval, my husband and I invited those who attended the funeral to our house for lunch, instead of the traditional church meal. I believe it was another fork in the road of my life. I had wondered: Should I sit back and watch from afar, as I had during my grandmother's funeral six years earlier, or should I attempt to comfort my family as they had comforted me so often over the years? Under my senior picture in my high school yearbook, it reads -- "*to be THERE when I am needed.*" My hope was that this choice would be consistent with that goal.

Mom's visitation was on New Year's Day. After the visitation, Linda and her family joined us for our traditional pork and sauerkraut meal to ring in the new year. It was a very special time together as we watched the Rose Bowl game pitting The Ohio State University Buckeyes against the Oregon Ducks. Grandma and Mom would have been cheering right along with us as they were passionate fans! Perhaps, in some celestial way, they were present. For three hours, we smiled and cheered as our team rolled to victory. Mom was a part of our conversation and we had fun as she would have wanted.

Mom's funeral occurred in the morning at the funeral home near her home. The pastor's words and scripture choices were meaningful, but my sister's words about our mom and her life touched my heart deeply. Again, it was just as Mom would have wanted it to be, honoring, with a sprinkle of humor intermixed to keep it light and celebratory.

After the funeral, family and friends gathered in our home for a luncheon provided by my dearest friends. This time together was not only healing for others, it was also healing for me. As that afternoon unfolded, each recollection of Mom became a treasure.

Some family members I had never met, and some of her friends didn't know I was her daughter. That was okay with me. To my knowledge, only one cousin asked another cousin if I was Linda's half-sister because of our similarities in appearance and mannerisms. He proceeded to tell her we were full sisters and that he had been introduced to me at a birthday party for our grandmother years earlier.

Later that year, those two cousins, with my sister and I began an in-depth journey into our family's genealogy. Former generations provided my sister and cousin valuable information that they had saved. Other family members provided additional facts as we dug deeper. Our *Copeland Mystery Tour* took us to six different cemeteries and two libraries in Ohio that year. We uncovered a plethora of interesting stories about our ancestors as well as establishing a unique bond of friendship that may not have evolved had we not met in our home after Mom's funeral. From my perspective, it was a rare opportunity to help build on the knowledge of our family's history for the next generation while developing a significant camaraderie with my cousins.

We continue to meet for lunch several times a year. Our group has expanded to include more of the family. As the years have passed, the rest of the family seems delighted that our collaboration has brought the generations together to share more information and answer questions as they continue to arise. Ancestry is rarely discussed, and extensive research did not resume until 2021 when we verified the information we had, added new discoveries, and created a family ancestry book with all the information that we gathered over the years. Thanks to Beth, the cousin who inquired as to my identity, our research was assembled into a book that was given to those who expressed an interest. It has provided a bit of comfort and pleasure to the older generation, knowing we are excited to keep our ancestry alive and pass it along to the next generation! It may be what has sparked more family gatherings. What a gift!

A few years back, a message thread began with cousins and aunts who are fans of the same college football team. Mom would be thrilled, since she loved the Buckeyes and would have been right in there during the games to contribute her "two cents." On game days, our phones are constantly chirping as we analyze what just happened on the field. We continue to learn more about each other as the conversation shifts from sports to family. Family members from Arizona, Indiana, Ohio, and Kentucky share memories and news that might otherwise be unknown due to the distance between us. My husband and I were honored to host an overnight stay in our home with some of our family, thanks to that thread and an inquiry from yet another cousin.

There have been bumps and potholes along my journey to finding the rest of me, and that is to be expected, I suppose. Each of us evolves, and our perspectives change as we age. At this crossroads, I am content to keep in mind whose I was on earth and whose I am in heaven. If anything gets in the way of seeking joy for the kingdom to come, I will politely pass and move on.

Who do I choose to remain loyal to as time progresses, as loved one's pass from this life, and the family configuration changes? The family dynamic is bound to modify over the years. To be intentional about staying in touch with my biological and my adoptive family has its challenges. This is a conundrum for those of us who were adopted and chose this path.

Until my last breath, I'm committed to both of my families – the one I was born into and the one that chose me. How that will look in the future may change, and that's okay, too.

I'm grateful for the privilege of sharing seventeen years on this earth with my birth mom. Now that God holds her soul in the hollow of His hand where she is forever protected, she lingers in my memories and my heart. He has promised our reunion, and I faithfully wait.

—Chapter 15—
Transitions

In spite of their twelve-year age difference, my birth mom, Barb, and my adoptive brother, Walt, had a few things in common. They were both a part of the Silent Generation, so named because they were raised during the Great Depression and WWII. Barb would be alive during both, whereas Walt was born after the Depression but lived with its lingering effects. The Silent Generation, children born from 1925-1945, were also called the Traditionalist Generation due to the fact that the majority worked hard within the system and kept their heads down, thus earning themselves the "silent" label. Although not blood kin, Barb and Walt shared attributes. Both were hard workers, but they were also risk-takers; neither leaned toward playing it safe or remaining silent.

Time has taught me that change happens to people, even if they don't like it or agree with it. On the other hand, a transition is internal. It takes place in people's minds as they go through changes. Change can come about very quickly, while transition usually occurs more slowly. Life shifts can be difficult. Transitions can be debilitating. One of the challenges of my life has been the reluctance to transition from baby to eldest child in the two families in which I have become a member. I am the youngest daughter in my adoptive family and the eldest daughter in my biological family. The roles would vacillate upon entering each family's world. The title changed quickly and forever on the day my brother, Walt, passed into his new life away from this earth.

I was ten years younger than my brother, and we were occasionally mistaken to be only children. Many of his friends knew little about me, and my friends seldom saw him since he went off to college when I was 8. In college, he lived for a time with our paternal grandparents so he knew them better than I. He brought home lots of stories but I cannot remember many of them. I was the "baby" of the family, and I wasn't expected to remember. After college, Walt returned to Lima as a married man and attended law school at Ohio Northern University. After receiving his Juris Doctor degree and passing the Ohio Bar exam, Walt began his law practice in our dad's office. Upon his arrival, he quickly became known as the young whippersnapper, a title he embraced. Because of their names, Walter M. Lawson, Jr., and Walter M. Lawson, III, there was always a bit of confusion in addressing them.

Dad was very methodical! After his passing, his peers met in a courtroom in the courthouse where a judge presided. All the attorneys, who were present, were given the floor to share their final thoughts about my father, their colleague and sometimes their adversary. All who spoke referred to his attention to detail. He would have no surprise in his briefcase, like Perry Mason. You knew what you were getting – and you had just better be prepared because he would be.

Walt, a recent law school graduate, was confident in his abilities and was quick to assess and give his opinion. Walt and my dad were both very smart, and their clients were pleased with both of them, but they were not pleased with each other. In my dad's opinion, Walt needed to dedicate more time to each case. Walt thought Dad spent far too much time deliberating over his cases. So my brother and his family packed up and began the adventure that would take them across the country. He became the legal superintendent for state mental health hospitals in a number of states. As this was a political position, he changed addresses according to which party was in power.

In 1996, ten years before my father's death, Walt returned home to work with him again. Walt had been actively involved in every community in which he'd resided, and his presence was highly valued. However, he was content to rejoin our dad during this season of their lives. Both had mellowed, and these were wonderful years for our family. The cousins had more opportunities to be together, as did their parents. I happily transitioned back into the role of baby of the family much of the time.

When Dad passed, we officially began the work of siblings. Walt took over the duties of the law office and I, being the executor of Dad's estate, took over the responsibility of executing his will. The same occurred after Mom's passing. Walt and I talked frequently and collaborated often. We completed their various requests a year after the passing of our mother.

We enjoyed almost two years of "normalcy" together. Then, Walt was diagnosed with basal tongue-squamous cell cancer the month Barb died! I transitioned, as best I could, between offering support to my sister-in-law for my older brother, and being available to comfort or offer assistance to my younger sister after our mother's passing!

Cancer is awful for everyone. It ravages your loved one's physical body and mental state, while destroying any shred of energy for those caring for and loving the one with cancer to concentrate on other aspects of life. Walt underwent chemo and radiation treatments for 10 months. He was in remission for 3 1/2 years. *Transitions*.

The following years were difficult for my brother and his family. My husband and I felt it, too. Anytime I picked up my computer to begin writing, I would think of Walt and lose interest. Thankfully, he was given a clean bill of health for several years. However, he continued to be monitored after his treatments were completed. During my brother's "reprieve" from cancer, my husband and I retired and moved away from our hometown, where we had lived for almost 60 years. We were ready for a change and wanted to live by a lake and enjoy the benefits of the calm waters of retirement.

However, we were resolved to remain active in both my adoptive and our biological families' lives. Our time was spent exploring our new surroundings, meeting new friends, and enjoying all who came to visit us. One day while unpacking, I found myself poring through the box labeled "adoption." I set it out so that I could begin to organize both the box and my thoughts regarding all that I had journaled and accumulated in the past twenty years. In October 2013, I received the dreadful call that my brother's cancer had returned, and I put it all away.

Walt was diagnosed with Stage 3 lung cancer, and he couldn't undergo radiation therapy due to its close proximity to the esophagus, where he had been treated for his other cancer. Through phone conversations and occasional visits, we observed the progression of his deteriorating health over the first regimen of chemotherapy and radiation therapy. He had to stop his chemotherapy when they discovered a squamous cell skin cancer on top of his head. Chemotherapy would not allow that cancer to heal after it was taken off his head. The plan was to switch chemotherapy after it had healed. On a warm sunny Sunday in November, Walt called to tell me that he was choosing not to undergo more chemo treatments. As sad as we were hearing the news, we respected his decision. He was tired and sick all of the time. His doctor told he might have six good months.

We were back home the following week to spend a few hours with him. He was too weak to visit but gave us a smile as we said our goodbyes. Our plan was to visit more often, but he only lived three more weeks. The cancer returned with a vengeance, and then he was gone. It was New Year's Day when my sister-in-law called to tell me his death was imminent. Our kids had just arrived, after a four and one-half hour trip from Ohio, and we were preparing to open Christmas gifts. I excused myself to our back deck, where I swept the wooden floors until I had no more tears to shed. Four and a half hours away, and his passing was imminent. I wanted to be in both places at once. This time I wanted to be the mom and the sister simultaneously.

Walt's four children and wife were around his bedside as he passed peacefully four hours later. I had chosen to remain in Somerset. I'll never know if he was waiting for his baby sister, but I had made the choice to transition into the role of mother and older sister. I think a little of me hoped if I stayed home, he would, too.

For a moment, my perception of the world shattered on the day my brother passed from this life. Our family of four was reduced to one. It felt reminiscent of concertos I'd performed as a cellist in orchestras over the years. The concerto begins with an uplifting, brisk and lively movement, resembling the fun-loving carefree moments of childhood and young adulthood. It proceeds to a slower, calm and lyrical movement, corresponding to adulthood with a career established and watching children grow up. The final movement is fast and lively, like the years of maturing adulthood, when the days feel long but the years whisk by relentlessly. The part leading up to the finale sometimes has a crescendo that feels like it could literally take you out of your seat. For a while, my life felt stuck in a crescendo of emotions that I couldn't release. My loved ones had become ill and passed far too quickly. I didn't have time to process one heartbreak before the next occurred.

A concerto is performed with a soloist accompanied by an orchestra to add support to the musical theme and texture to the soloist. I felt like the soloist, but I could no longer hear the orchestra. My orchestra was the Lawson family, and it had been silenced by death. An orphan again. This time, I knew it, and it felt lonely. My husband was always close by to offer emotional support, but it was often difficult to put my emotions into words.

During the painful moments, I went to our local equestrian therapy program where I volunteered, and hugged my favorite horse until my tears subsided. At times, I longed for the second movement, the calm and clarity of knowing who I was and whose I was. And then, I remembered. All along, God was there just as I wanted to be there for those I love. God's promises have been meaningful for my entire life. "I will not leave you orphans: I will come to you" (New King James Version Bible, 1983, John 14:18). What a precious promise for adoptees! Nothing had changed with Him. He still was and would always be with me. I just needed to remember.

Walt's was a hard goodbye that haunts me to this day. It's been eight years and a great sadness still penetrates my heart every time I think of him. I suppose my heart is having trouble catching up with my head. I'm the one who is left to recall the stories and remind the younger generation of what wonderful family members preceded them. Humans are fortunate, in that we possess the ability to pass along the legacy of our forefathers and foremothers, essentially keeping those ancestors alive.

My brother's passing created a feeling of urgency I've not felt before. I am now embracing my new role of family historian, and I enjoy opening up the old family photo albums and delighting in the memories they evoke. I relish the opportunities to share the stories I still remember with my nieces, nephews, and my own children. I am fully aware that they may need to be repeated, and there will not be enough time for me to tell them often enough. It's a challenging role, but I have already begun to compose the special stories as I remember them.

Passing from this life is not an ending. Our souls continue. It's just a transition!

Part III:
The Side Trip Along The Way

—Chapter 16—
Home - A Providential, Protected Property

In 2017, two years after my brother passed, I felt that familiar nudge once again. I pulled out the tri-fold pamphlet, my journals, the official documents and the other information I'd set aside so many years earlier. As I read through the trifold, I became determined to find out about my birth place and whether it still existed.

On April 17, 2017, I began looking online for information pertaining to unwed mother's homes in Columbus, Ohio. I quickly discovered that during the years when the Friends Rescue Home was in operation, at least one other maternity home existed in Columbus, and it was called the Florence Crittenton Home for Unwed Mothers. It was founded in 1883, by Charles Nelson Crittenton, a wealthy New York merchant. He opened the first mission home in New York City in memory of his daughter, Florence, who had died at the age of four. The purpose of this home was to reform "fallen women" by preaching salvation and providing shelter for unmarried, pregnant women and girls. Crittenton became a traveling evangelist, preaching to prostitutes and unwed mothers.

From the Friends Home trifold, it appeared that the Quakers had a similar purpose. I had to look deeper, but didn't know where to begin.

Friends Rescue Home. Who was being rescued? It didn't make sense to me. Why was this place, considered by my mother to be a place of extreme judgment, called a rescue home?

I went back online and typed in the words Friends Rescue Home to see if there was documentation regarding its existence. I discovered an online report detailing the first ten years of the Friends Rescue Home on North Harris Avenue. "The Home opened in 1905 by Evangeline Reams. It was a home for wayward girls and unprotected children. It provided food, clothing and shelter for unwed mothers and other at risk youth." Amazing! It made sense that rescue fit between Friends and Home. It was a safe haven for at-risk girls, children and unwed mothers. They were being rescued from those who might cause harm to this vulnerable group in the early 1900s.

I learned that in 1916, the Home moved from Harris to 278 and 283 E. 13th Street, to accommodate their growing population. Those two homes would become too small, and 219 North Chase Avenue, which became 245 North Powell Avenue, was the final residence for the Friends Rescue Home.

My search continued. On Facebook, I discovered a site named Franklin County Genealogical and Historical Society. I found a thread on that site that led me to another site called Historical West Side. This particular page offers individuals an opportunity to share facts and engage in discussions about the history of that area of Columbus, Ohio. While scrolling down the page, I recognized a photo of an old home with a tall signpost and the words FRIENDS RESCUE HOME, 245 N. Powell, in the foreground. It looked like it was taken in the 1960s, judging from the clothing worn by the ladies walking toward the home. The Home matched the one pictured on the front of the Friends Home pamphlet I found in my dad's dresser, and the address on my original birth certificate. Indeed, it was, and I was delighted!

On that site, a dialogue related to the Home began in 2013. Most of the questions and comments pertained to individuals whose family members had spent time in the home while pregnant. They were searching for answers about themselves, their birth mothers, and other family members. More than halfway through the comments, a message appeared that literally brought me out of my seat with a gasp.

A man identified the location as being the property his parents purchased in 1979, and he stated that some of his family still lived on the premises. I had to remember that this conversation was four years old. As soon as I regained my composure, I sat back down and began the task of locating him on Facebook, sending him a personal message and a friend request. I don't think my fingers ever typed so quickly and with so few mistakes. I knew exactly what I wanted to ask. I told him that the reason for my interest in connecting with him was similar to the others who had posted comments four years earlier. I was interested in knowing about the place where I was born, if it still existed, and whether I was permitted to see it.

I went on to tell him I lived in Somerset, Kentucky, but I had family in Columbus and would welcome the opportunity to drive up if his family was receptive. He responded immediately by telling me he would send my inquiry to his sister who lived there, and that I should contact her directly. His family still owned and operated the Christian Conference Center, formerly the Friends Rescue Home. He felt confident that my questions would be welcomed.

This was not the first time an adoptee had contacted his family and he was certain his sister would be open to sharing what she knew. She and her husband, as well as his mother, were currently living on the property in another house behind the Home. He told me that his sister's oldest son and his family resided in a third home on the property. I was a bit shocked, to say the least. How easy, like finding my biological mother. But, then again, I was following God's lead, not my own. I should have known that He would open the appropriate window at the correct time. This day was almost 25 years from the day I first initiated contact with my biological mother.

These were the words I wrote to his sister, who was named Blythe Ann.

"Hi! I just received a message from your brother. He indicated that he was sending my inquiry to you and that it was okay for me to reach out to you. I was born at the Friends Rescue Home in 1954. I met my biological mother when I was 38 years old. I felt God's 'nudge' to express my gratitude to her. My life has been so full -- an amazing and wonderful adoptive family as well as the opportunity to meet and love my biological family. Many in my biological and adoptive families have passed, and I am feeling that 'nudge' to dig deeper and write about it all. I would sincerely appreciate the opportunity to come visit the home my biological mom spoke about years ago. Is it possible to make arrangements to visit? I currently live in Kentucky but I visit the Columbus area frequently, as I have family living there. Thank you for your consideration of my request."

I am not normally this bold but decided I should give her a full picture of my expectations and let her decide if she was willing.

The sister's response was immediate and definitive. "Jan, you are always welcome to come 'home'. We'll work out whatever time you want to travel."

Imagine my delight and giddiness upon hearing this news, within minutes of sending her my inquiry at 10:26 P. M. Home. She called it home. She made it sound so warm and welcoming. Immediately, I thanked her! Our friendship took root that evening and continues to flourish.

Blythe Ann and I corresponded many times before we met in person. Once was on Saturday, April 22nd, the 25th anniversary of contacting my biological mother, Barb, for the first time. The initial date we were considering for a visit didn't work out.

Soon afterward, I encountered another God nudge regarding the possibility of inviting my sister to accompany me to the Home. I contacted Blythe Ann, and she graciously accepted my request, but my sister was reluctant when I invited her to join me. Thoughtfully, she told me it was my story. I reminded her that Barb was our mom and that this was our story, not just mine. She eventually agreed, and I was both relieved and happy.

Several more dates were discussed, but they had to be postponed because of sickness or more serious health issues that needed to be addressed immediately. At one point, we wondered if this meeting would transpire. However, each piece of correspondence between

Blythe Ann and me gave me reason to believe this meeting was not fortuitous, but meant to be. Perseverance paid off.

Eight months after our original contact, a date and time became available for us to be introduced.

This gem of a structure came to life that day. Twenty-five years had passed from the moment I first held my original birth certificate indicating where I'd been born. My birth mother's comments gave meaning to its existence. Ten years had passed from the moment of my first glimpse of my birthplace, on a tattered, gold-colored paper, tri-fold pamphlet tucked away in my father's dresser drawer. The trifold added depth to the original intent of the Home. The thought that this Home might continue to exist and serve others brought a new enthusiasm to my search. Now I had the opportunity to walk up the steps and through the threshold of this majestic home with my sister. Within those walls, I would not only find where my mother and I met but discover more priceless blessings, off the beaten path, on my journey to finding the rest of me.

Kay Armstrong Unverzagt. (1960's). *Friends Rescue Home.* [photograph]. Columbus, Ohio. (Photo copied with permission from Kay Armstrong Unverzagt.)

Ohio Yearly Meeting of Friends. (n.d.) Friends Rescue Home front porch [Photograph]. Friends Rescue Home. (Photo copied with permission from the Archives Committee of Malone University and representatives from EFC-ER.)

Jan Schiffer. (2017). Christian Conference Center. [Photograph]. Columbus, Ohio.

—Chapter 17—
The Introduction to My First Home

During the years we first got acquainted, Barb's typical animated, energetic countenance had vanished whenever I mentioned the Home, and in its place a frown appeared. Any acts of generosity and kindness demonstrated by the women who worked there were overshadowed by the judgment she felt when she resided there. She was not permitted to smoke, and was frequently told that her body was no longer her own. Her freedom of movement was stifled and she was unhappy with the routine that she had to endure. She had been on her own, living with friends since she was sixteen years old, and her time had been free when she wasn't working. Then, at twenty-one, she found herself alone and pregnant with a married man's baby. Strangers were in charge of her care, and they were declaring the rules of engagement.

This described my birth mother's experience at the Home in 1953-1954. On Saturday, December 16th, 2017, I would forge a new relationship with this historic Home and its current residents. It felt like a connection I was destined to establish. All "roads" had led me there, and every part of my being was filled with hopeful anticipation.

My hands felt clammy on the steering wheel, and my heart was racing as my sister and I drove closer to our destination. I recall wondering how it would all play out. Blythe Ann seemed so amenable every time she communicated with me. There were no red flags to indicate I should feel anything other than optimistic.

We noticed that the streets surrounding Powell Avenue consisted of traditional one and one-half story homes with front porches the length of the house, and small, Cape Cod-style homes. As Linda and I made our way from the intersection of Ridge Ave. and Powell Ave., we realized the lane was leading us to a large, stately country home that was nothing like the rest of the block. This sprawling property of 8.1 acres was down a significant lane and set back from the intersecting street. A century ago, it had been a country estate, but now neighbors, whose homes were perhaps 350 yards to the south of the Home, occupied that space, and it had become a residential district.

After turning onto the paved lane, we drove across a guard railed bridge, with a barely trickling creek bed, whose stream of water eventually made its way to the beautiful Scioto River. As we reached the circular drive, I was immediately captivated by the impressive English Tudor-style home. Palpable excitement flushed through my body as I took in this grand structure for the first time. I was intrigued by the makeshift street sign pole with two standard green metal street markers and a 5-mph sign at the base of it. The long lane was designated Francis Marion Drive, while the intersecting sign was labeled Blythe Circle. I wondered who these names referred to, and their significance to the current inhabitants. We were impressed with the elegant old oak and buckeye trees within the semi-circle driveway, which in full bloom, probably obstructed the lovely view of the house.

After I stepped out of my car, I took a good look at the Home in front of me. It possessed a steeply pitched roof with several overlapping windowed gables, two tall ornate stone and masonry chimneys and chimney pipes (metal pipes appearing at the top). The groupings of windows, with one set having the characteristic Tudor-style of exposed wood frames, were filled with stucco.

As Linda and I ascended the four steps to the front porch, we remarked about the outside appearance of the Home, and I imagined how it might have looked in its heyday, and in our mom's era. The first-floor exterior was stone/masonry while the second and third floors were a combination of dark brown timber and plaster.

I could hardly take my eyes off the craftsmanship of this elegant old mansion and began to imagine the history it held within its walls. The workmanship of the burnt orange/clay square tile porch floor was remarkable. Most may not feel a sense of exhilaration as they glance at the place of their birth. But sixty-three years after my arrival in this world, visiting this structure was a goosebumps moment for me. This was my first home, and I couldn't wait to see any rooms we might be shown.

As we approached the steps to the porch, we noticed two stone pillars, on either end with large round white pillars perfectly spaced in the middle. Beside the steps was a wooden railing. Once on the porch, I felt compelled to look to the left where I remembered our mother describing the path that she had taken to begin her daily routine of walking around the property. The concrete sidewalk was still there, and more wooden railings were placed to the right of the walkway. I noticed a huge firepit and shelter house beyond the walkway to the right. I don't recall my mother mentioning either of those, so maybe that was new when the Hitch family purchased the property. But all the rest felt strangely familiar. Mom had described it well.

The smile on our hostess's face as she opened the door put me at ease immediately. Blythe Ann had presented her family's home many times, and she welcomed us in with a hug. I would soon discover that we were the same age and had a great deal in common. Oddly enough, I felt right at home from the moment we walked through the threshold. Everything about my experience would be different from my birth mom's. The season of my life, the circumstances surrounding my presence there, and the people who now occupied the space were all in stark contrast to what she had experienced as a young, unwed mother being greeted by people with whom she had no prior knowledge. A part of me longed for her presence on this part of my journey, but then I remembered her disparaging comments and understood this was an experience meant for me, not her. At that moment, I was grateful for my sister's willingness to accompany me.

Upon entering the Home, I noticed two sets of staircases in front of me, directly across from the front door. Each step on the right side held at least one Santa, all were unique and of varying sizes. We were escorted to the living room, on the left, where we were introduced to Blythe Ann's mother, Blythe Hitch, the matriarch of the family. We were told that she and her husband, Francis Marion Hitch, had purchased the property on a land contract from Buck Patton in 1979. The mystery regarding the names on the street pole had been uncovered.

After a short conversation with her mother, Blythe Ann escorted us into the dining room, to the right of the stairs, where she told us the rich history of the Home and its owners. Initially, U.S. Naval Commander John Holley Roys had the house built for his family. His wife, Emma Sullivant Rogers, was the great-granddaughter of Lucas Sullivant who founded Franklinton, Ohio, in 1797. Franklinton is less than 4 minutes away from the Home. At the time of their marriage in 1902, she was a widow with two children. Commander Roys was Vice Admiral William S. Sims' liaison officer with British Intelligence. During his naval career in England, he took a liking to Tudor architecture, and commissioned Frank Packard, a prominent architect in Ohio, to design an English Tudor-era styled country home for his wife and family.

The groundbreaking was in 1897, one hundred years after Emma Roys' great-grandfather had settled the area nearby. The home was completed in 1905. I'm told his wife considered it too opulent and it was eventually put up for sale. In 1918, it was sold to the Ohio Yearly Meeting of the Friends Church, and became the Friends Rescue Home. The Powell Avenue Friends Rescue Home provided housing, spiritual guidance, health care, and life skills for at-risk girls, as well as unwed mothers, from 1918 until 1971. The Quakers held conferences, retreats, camps and club meetings until 1978, when it was purchased by Buck Patton and his wife while she was in the process of beginning Hospice of Columbus.

Blythe Ann proceeded to tell us that her mother was introduced to the Home in 1979 during a conference being held at 245 North Powell Avenue. She went on a tour of the property and learned it was for sale. Nine years earlier, she and her husband were called to serve at the Hillcrest Baptist Church, which was less than a mile away. The Hitch family had a singing ministry and they'd been praying for a location where all the extended families could live and do ministry together. This property appeared to fill all of their needs.

In August, 1979, the Hitch family purchased the 5,108 square foot home, and the Christian Conference Center began its 40-year ministry on the Hilltop. The Center was used for conferences, training, seminars, and church and family gatherings. For 35 years, the family was actively involved in a music ministry group called The Hitches. They performed in many states and had several albums produced during that time.

In the summer of 1980, the Myti Oaks Daycamp commenced. It was a weekly summer experience for neighborhood children from kindergarten through 8th grade. Their mission statement was, "From tiny acorns mighty oaks grow." The program included musical, drama, sports training, and leadership development. After 38 years of the camp ministry, it closed in the summer of 2018. In 2016, they had partnered with an organization called the Coalition of Christian Outreach to establish an intentional Christian community living space for college students. The Hitch family lived in the Home for 31 years before moving into the ranch house behind the Home. In 2021, it was sold to a gentleman whose mission was to provide recovery and restoration for convicted men who had been recently released, as well as those recovering from addictions.

When my sister and I visited the Home in December 2017, it was called the Discipleship House. There were several college-aged young women living in a room that had been the labor and delivery room during the unwed mother's home era.

Next, we were taken on an extensive tour of the entire Home. We learned each room's purpose during the Friends Rescue Home years and the changes made during the Hitch years leading up to 2017. What an impressive history!

After our memorable tour, we were shown an old, framed picture [see below] that had been taken in front of the home in 1925, when it was being operated by the Quakers as a rescue home. It was taken to commemorate the 20th year of the Friends Rescue Home's existence.

There were 63 individuals (3 children, 50 adult women and 10 adult men) photographed together in this extraordinary 1925 photo. If those voices could be heard today, what an account they could provide for us of the Home's existence in those early years and their mission to help women and girls in need. This photo represented a little over the first third of the Friends Rescue Home's history, since it operated as an unwed mother's home until 1971.

It was at this juncture that a full circle moment occurred. I asked Blythe Ann if there might be others who could shed more light on the history of the Home during the unwed mother's home years. The one name she kept coming back to was "Clarkie." She said his last name was Clark but that everyone called him this. She said he'd be a wealth of knowledge, since he was part of the Religious Society of Friends and also the Home's ministry to the girls.

During that conversation, my sister mentioned that she had worked in a school down the street with a lady with the same last name, and that her family was part of the same meeting for worship. Imagine my excitement to think that my sister was not only part of my history, but part of this ever-growing connection to the story of this providential Home.

Several years after our visit, I had a phone conversation with my sister Linda's colleague, and it was revealed that her father was known as Clarkie. He had passed away years earlier. Another remarkable connection as a result of this "side trip." Of all the school districts my sister could have been associated with during her career in Columbus, it was Hilltonia Middle School, just minutes away from the Home after it became the Christian Conference Center in 1979. She probably had students who had attended their Myti Oaks Daycamp in the summer!

Additionally, another one of my sister's colleagues was actively involved in the summer musical ministry at the Home during the Christian Conference Center years. I had the good fortune to speak with her one day. She shared some interesting stories of the musicals that were performed by the neighborhood children who attended the summer camps when she was volunteering there.

Friends Rescue Home 20th Anniversary (Photo of framed 1925 photograph copied with permission from the Archives Committee of Malone University and representatives from EFC-ER.)

—Chapter 18—
Tours And Correspondences

There was no way to contain my enthusiasm the moment Blythe Ann had offered to take us on a tour of the house. Eagerly, I shook my head yes as I popped up from my chair in the dining room. My heart started racing, but not as rapidly as my mind. Mom hadn't shared much about the inside of the Home, but what she told me was firmly set to memory. I lapped it up like a thirsty dog enjoying a fresh bowl of water after a long walk in the hot summer sun. I assumed I would never see the Home in a picture, let alone walk through its hallways and up its staircases, so I was eager to have an image firmly planted in my mind's eye.

From the dining room, our hostess escorted Linda and me to the entryway where two sets of steps ascended in front of us. The remainder of the steps were singular staircases placed above and below the double stairs. The descending stairs led to the only public restroom and the room that housed the superintendent when my birth mother was living there. The ascending stairs led us to a landing with two rooms, side by side, and across from the second staircase. An additional three steps were required to enter either of those rooms. The room on the left housed the resident nurse, and the smaller room was the doctor's office. Most of the time there was a second nurse on site, too. She slept on the third floor in a room near the unwed mothers.

In 1911, the former Friends Rescue Home residence established a certified birthing center within its walls so that women would not have to leave the home to have their babies and then return. As a licensed maternity hospital, it was incorporated under the laws of Ohio and received the necessary papers from the Board of State Charities and the State Board of Health. Through an arrangement with the OSU College of Medicine, obstetrical work was handled by the head of the obstetrics department. The Home received a certain amount of money from the state for each case in return for the privilege of performing clinical work there.

Many original birth certificates, as well as amended birth certificates, have the name Dr. Francis W. Davis listed as the attending physician. He was an OSU assistant professor of Obstetrics in the College of Medicine and a Clinical Assistant Professor of Obstetrics and Gynecology in the mid 1930s into the late 1960s. Dr. Davis donated his obstetrical services to the Home for over 30 years. He delivered or supervised the delivery of all babies born during that time. Dr. Davis's signature is on both of my birth certificates.

After climbing the middle staircase to the second floor, we were introduced to the labor and delivery room. Sixty-three years after I first entered the world, I was standing in the same labor and delivery room where the miracle of birth had occurred many times. On February 28, 1954, it was my life that was ushered in here, and I was awestruck by the magnitude of emotion I felt in that moment. My birth mother had shared impressions of that cold dreary day many times over the years, and I was trying to remember them.

When we visited this room, it was set up for what female college students might require, since that is who lived in the room. The young women were aware of the room's purpose during the Friends Rescue Home years, and I wondered if they ever thought about all the precious lives that began there.

It all seemed so unreal to me, and I wanted to linger long enough to envision how it might have looked, but Blythe Ann and my sister had already headed down the hallway to another room. Instead, I took a picture and moved on.

Next, we were led into the recovery/convalescing room, where Mom had felt the warmth from a toasty fire in the fireplace. There was no longer a fireplace in the room, and its contents looked nothing like I'd imagined. It had been removed in the late 50s, during a remodel, but I could reproduce it in my mind from pictures I had seen from the 1920s and 1930s.

For a moment, I stopped to imagine what my birth mom might have been feeling that afternoon. At 21 years of age, she had just given birth to her first child without family around her. They were miles away. No one who really knew her was there to congratulate her on a healthy delivery, or to console her after she held her new baby girl. She was alone.

While it was exciting for me to pass over the threshold into the room of my beginning, it was sad to imagine my mom's pain. My eyes filled with tears as I considered the chasm of emotions, both hers then, and mine now. It was at that moment that my mother's sacrifice was made abundantly clear to me.

As we ascended the final staircase to the third floor, my memories of Mom's recollection of the numerous stairs to the "barracks" came flooding back. She told me it felt safe to be on the top floor with the other girls. She described her chores and how difficult it had become to walk up all those steps near the end of her pregnancy. As I peered out of the third story window, I wondered how often she had looked out, and what she might have thought about as she dragged her weary body up to bed at night. Thirty-three steps to reach her bedroom, which was a converted attic. What were her thoughts in the morning as she descended the staircases to the dining room?

Years earlier, the large room on the third floor had contained eighteen metal framed twin beds with a chair on the side of the bed. Underneath each chair was a small, washable cotton rug. Down the "hallway" there was a wall filled with eighteen tiny closets! Mercifully, there was a bathroom on that floor, but only one for all those girls. In those days, only one full bathroom was normal in most homes. A friend of mine once told me that her eleven-member family figured out how to share one full bathroom for years.

When we visited, there were no beds, chairs or any other remnants of a dormitory. Instead, the room was lined with sheets of drywall, drop cloths, a pile of 2" x 4" wood, a large selection of tools, and a ladder. Endless amounts of work to be completed in order to renovate for potential future occupancy. It looked like an overwhelming task to me.

We took the doctor's stairs down to the main floor. There was a separate set of "back" stairs that were not available to anyone other than the doctor or the nurse. The residents would only see the doctor on the third floor, or perhaps in his office near the stairway. There was a side entrance near the kitchen where he could enter and leave the building discreetly. It was astonishing to consider how perfectly appointed this home was for its purpose as a home and hospital.

It felt bittersweet saying good-bye to these engaging ladies, but they had spent most of their afternoon with us and we'd been given such a gift – a valuable history lesson and a tour of this amazing home. After taking a few photos to commemorate our visit, we expressed our gratitude and hugged both women before walking out the front door. Upon leaving, my sister and I lingered a bit longer to take in the walkway where the unwed mothers walked for their daily exercise. We walked around the circular drive and back to our car in silence.

It is a humbling feeling to step into the hallowed doorway of one's birthing room. That day, I was so happy that my sister had chosen to come with me. She would be the only person who could fill a part of the vast void I was feeling. Oh, how I wished Mom could have been there at that moment to reflect on it all. More unanswered questions would follow in the weeks that followed. My birth mother had valued my life enough to go through a pregnancy and healthy delivery, and that is all that really matters.

My journal entry on December 16, 2017 reads:

Today I stood in the room where my life began. I thought it might feel like a "full circle" experience. It did not because the one who carried me and gave me life was no longer by my side, and her absence is now even more poignant. So many questions left unanswered. The room's purpose has changed but I could imagine the emotion of all of those births as I attempted to picture the past. The area where a fireplace once stood caught my attention almost immediately upon entering the room. My mother recalled being warmed by a fire in the recovery room after I was born that cold February afternoon. So many years ago! The large windows were now covered with lightweight brown curtains. I wonder what the coverings were on the day of my arrival. Were they opened or closed on that winter day? I chuckled as I noted the old upright doctor's scales which were still a part of the room's "landscape". I wanted to linger but my sister and I were guests and our hostess was anxious to show us the remainder of the house. Someday, I hope to go back and tarry a bit longer. I would like to return to take a picture of the place where my eyes first opened on this earth.

After that first meeting, I stayed in touch with Blythe Ann over the next two months, occasionally asking questions, but mostly wishing to stay connected with my new friend.

On February 5, 2018, at 9:19 AM, I received this note from her.

"Good morning, Jan. I think about you and your sister often. It was such a great visit the day you came - and you should be glad, too. But not for what you think. We had a pipe burst in the shower room, on the third floor, about 6 weeks ago. The water ran for 6-8 hours - best guess. Second floor apartment, labor and delivery rooms have to be gutted. The kitchen was gutted last Saturday. It's a mess. But, of course, we're moving forward. Thank you for continuing to ask about me and mama. Your story is amazing - especially after 26 years. I'm glad we're a part of it. Blessings my friend."

I would not return to the Christian Conference Center/Discipleship House until June 30, 2019. Blythe Ann and I communicated, but not frequently. From Valentine's Day 2018 until June 26th of the following year, our only contact was through Messenger or occasional posts on Facebook.

On my visit in 2019, it was a beautiful, warm sunny afternoon, as opposed to the rather gloomy December day when Linda and I first drove up to the Home. Green grass covered the grounds and the mature oak and buckeye trees were filled with leaves, providing privacy and shade. I walked up the steps to the porch with a huge smile on my face before ever seeing Blythe Ann's face as she opened the door with her familiar smile. She and I were like old friends with so many hours of written conversation between us. It was good to see her again.

We embraced and she immediately led me to the kitchen where we sat and chatted for over 45 minutes before heading up the stairs. I was anxious to begin photographing all the rooms that we hurriedly walked through on our initial visit. This time would be different. As I entered each room, I continued to possess a sense of familiarity but my feelings were more layered, more complex.

Now, the ever-evolving story of the Home was more complicated to unravel. In 2017, I knew very little about it beyond what was in the trifold pamphlet and what Blythe Ann had shared with me. Two days before my second visit, I acquired an additional perspective from a woman who lived at the FRH during her pregnancy in 1969. I found it sad, but enlightening, that Lynn's impression of the Home was remarkably similar to that of my biological mother. Fifteen years later and still the same perception. We had several conversations that year, and each time I felt more unsettled about my "delighted" feeling. This new information caused me to make a conscious effort to become more acquainted with the social mores, norms and values of the 1950s when my birth mom was there.

According to the pamphlet from Friends Rescue Home in 1926, the hope was to save betrayed, erring and outcast girls. "They are not, as so many think, of low moral standards, but for the most part they are victims of misplaced confidence, unwholesome environments and thoughtless actions of the "Jazz" age." My mother arrived at the Home during the Baby Scoop era (1945-1970).

"The Baby Scoop Era was a period in United States history starting after the end of World War II and ending in approximately 1972, characterized by an increased rate of premarital pregnancies over the preceding period, along with a higher rate of newborn adoption." It was during the Baby Scoop Era that sentiment shifted from betrayed, erring and outcast girls to illegitimacy as a psychological deficit on the part of the mother. The dominant psychological and social work view was that the large majority of unmarried mothers were better off being separated by adoption from their newborn babies. A liberalization of sexual mores combined with restrictions on access to birth control led to an increase in premarital pregnancies.

By 1968, the fundraising pamphlet from the Home stated that the mission was to comfort the anguish and sorrow of the young and troubled girls – new life, new hope, new ideals and friendship.

In the 50s, it was common to assume that a young girl's goal in life was to assume the composite role of sweetheart, wife and mother. The highlight of a woman's life was her wedding day. This was considered the post-World War II gender norm for a female. A career was only for the truly ambitious, and those who thought outside the proverbial box. Nursing and teaching were the exceptions. Therefore, it is no wonder that the unwed mother felt judged by strangers whom they saw as not knowing anything about them beyond the fact that they often carried the burden of pregnancy alone.

These girls and women were not following the script, and society had alerted the masses about the need to "tuck them away" so that they might become worthy of marriage after they were no longer pregnant. They were shunned and maternity homes were in vogue.

On the other hand, the birth father was not considered a prodigal without redemption. Rather, he was sowing his wild oats and quickly, quietly forgiven. It is no surprise that my birth mom struggled with society's judgment of her, including those who were caring for her in the Home.

My perception of the Home was quite different from my birth mother and friend, Lynn, but I didn't walk through the doors as an unwed mother in the 50s or 60s. Society's opinion of the unwed mother had shifted considerably by 2017. A pregnant woman had options, thanks to all the revisions in women's health care over the past 65 years. A change in societal norms has altered the stigma of the unwed mother significantly over the years, as well. What once was shunned and hidden is no longer frowned upon by the secular community. Rather, it has become an acceptable choice, or so our country's legislative decisions appear to confirm.

My reason for walking through that door was to experience what was brought to light in the trifold and through my birth mother's experience. It was a very one-dimensional purpose that led me there initially. I was warmly welcomed and given a rich history of the compassionate people occupying this rather sacred space. It wasn't until my visit in 2019 that I was privy to the Home's original purpose and how it had evolved over the years.

As for the house, a great deal of change had taken place in the one and one-half years since I first visited, mostly due to the water leak originating in the bathroom on the third floor. There was a lot of remodeling underway when I arrived. From the kitchen, we walked to the hallway behind the dining room, and passed the private stairs which were meant for only the physician and nurses. I continued down the hall to the doctor's side entrance beside the kitchen, and peered out the window briefly. I knew this visit would be a more reflective one for me. I wondered how the young resident students had been prepped for this unique experience, and how they felt as they entered the side door. As I turned around and walked down the same hallway, I imagined the kitchen staff prepping for the next meal on the other side of the wall. Mere footsteps from one another, both caring for the needs of the unwed mothers.

As I turned to ascend the next set of steps leading up to the second floor, I thought about Dr. Davis, the physician who donated his obstetrical services to the Home for thirty years. This place must have felt so familiar to him, but I wondered how he felt about the women he was serving and the service he was providing for them at the time. How many emotional secrets did he have to keep locked away on the shelf of confidentiality? On each floor and in each room, I took my time taking photographs and writing down pertinent information regarding the room and its contents then, and now.

College-aged young men had replaced the young women who had occupied the rooms in 2017. I found it incredibly difficult to believe that this Home had ever had any other purpose than that of an accredited hospital within a home for unwed mothers. Flawlessly appointed rooms and hallways for discretionary visits.

Upon leaving, Blythe Ann informed me that she needed to leave for an appointment, but invited me to take my time walking around the exterior of the Home, which I did. I thought it was my final visit and I wanted to soak it all in. I felt fortunate to have seen the property in the winter and the summer. The mature trees made a remarkable difference in the Home's stately appearance.

All that I had learned about the Home in the past two years was significant, but I found myself wanting more facts, more insights into its past, more stories of those who entered its doorway and walked up its steps. On the three and one-half hour drive back home, I was torn between the joy of having discovered this providential place and sadness in realizing the door of opportunity might be closing quickly, and I may never have another chance to see it. There was talk of the dwelling's repair work becoming too overwhelming physically, as well as financially. I understood what that meant. The current owners had made a valiant effort over the years, but the setbacks were now extreme, and there were no longer as many hands, or finances, to keep up with the necessary repair work.

Fortunately for me, there was a third visit in the Home on December 9, 2020. It was a week shy of the three-year anniversary of my initial visit and one and one-half years from my last visit. Two note-worthy events had occurred in the last few months leading up to my final visit. The matriarch, Blythe Ann's sweet mother, entered into her eternal home, and the Home and property around it had been sold. There would be a continuation of ministry in this "protected, providential property on the Hilltop" as Blythe Ann referred to it. The gentleman who purchased the property has a cleaning business that provides an opportunity for men who are recently released from incarceration and those recovering from addictions to learn life skills to help them pursue a confident, productive future.

I contacted Blythe Ann when I saw her mother's obituary, and again when I read that the house was up for sale. I thought it very generous of her to invite me for one last visit. She and her family had the insurmountable task of clearing out all of the years of ministry and personal belongings this huge home had housed in preparation for the next owners. She told me she welcomed my visit because she had taken all of the old brochures and a book about Evangeline Reams, the founder of the Friends Rescue Home, out of the safe and wanted to give me an opportunity to look through them and the house one last time. Once she told me I was the only adoptee who came to visit who "stuck." I stayed in touch and had a desire to return again. She said she wanted me to possess the rich history should I follow through with writing a book one day.

It was so good to see my friend again. It was a different experience because we were in the midst of the Covid pandemic. I was coming from Kentucky, and we discussed the pros and cons of such a meeting during this vulnerable time. We chose to meet anyway and made a plan to be cautious of our space. I was surprised to see she had other company as I walked in the front door. Blythe Ann introduced me to a couple who had come by for a visit, too.

The woman had worked at the Home during the Hitch era, and she and her husband had become good friends of the family. We sat around a table as Blythe Ann began sharing the Friends Rescue Home's years of brochures and pamphlets she had taken from the safe. The pictures captivated my attention as did the frequent comments from her guests. It was interesting to hear their perspective of the Christian Conference Center and other programs that existed when they were there. I could have listened to their stories all day long, but knew my time was limited. I excused myself from the table.

I took my time exploring each room of the house one last time. This time I was alone, rather appropriate considering my emotions were all over the place. There were lots of boxes scattered about in each room, as one has when emptying a house. I barely noticed them. My mind raced to another time – when young, frightened girls were walking through the threshold of the front door for the first time, or trudging up those stairs with the extra weight of a baby inside them. Breathless and in need of rest before the next sunrise. Mothers-to-be who were deep in thought about this moment in their lives, and what the next season of their existence would look like. Souls that were saved thanks to the faithful followers of Jesus who came to share the good news with them.

I presume my mother had profound thoughts regarding her yesterdays, as well as looking ahead to her tomorrows, but I know she was unwilling to surrender her soul or ignite her inner light as desired for her by those in ministry. They were strangers in charge of enforcing strict rules, and had appeared to have little compassion for her circumstances. She felt their judgment, however unreal it might have been. Her entire world felt like a place of judgment, but she dealt with it because of the love she felt from and for her family. She merely existed in the Home in order to deliver her baby and leave. She had no desire to carry any part of this place with her. Perhaps she wondered how different her life would now be having been pregnant—having been here—having felt alone while among others like herself. Others may have obtained new skills and a faith to catapult them into a better life once they walked out the door. She would have none of it.

Whether they were toting their baby or just their bags, the Religious Society of Friends (Quakers) started this mission to save the whole girl/woman, which included her soul. They felt led by God to this mission field of giving hope, and providing a safe delivery for these young women. God nudges are powerful. In spite of the toll I knew it took on my mother and many like her, the Friends original purpose was successful for many of the unwed mothers in their nearly 70 years of service. I find that amazing!

Before leaving, Blythe Ann gave me one of the yearly brochures created to solicit funds for the Home, and permitted me to borrow the book about the founder and several other brochures and pamphlets. The only condition was that I return them before the house closed, so that she could give them to the new owners. She wanted the next occupants to have the history.

As in past visits, I took my time leaving that day. I walked around the circle, down near the lane parallel to the Camp Chase trail, and the abandoned tracks of the Cincinnati and Lake Erie Railway. Years ago on a warm afternoon, one would see a plethora of sheets and pillowcases hanging from the series of outdoor clotheslines that would take up much of the side yard. Imagine the amount of laundry. There was a time when chickens were freely running about the yard, as well. As there were never enough eggs or chickens to feed the girls, the Friends from Ypsilanti, Michigan, would send them a flock around Thanksgiving every year.

In years past, a resident groundskeeper/gardener had kept the grounds immaculate with a colorful English flower garden in addition to a fruit and vegetable garden. The garden provided the residents with fresh produce in the summertime and canned vegetables and fruit in the winter. Mom was there in the winter and would have enjoyed the canned goods, but she never mentioned it.

As I walked back to my car, I thought about Mom and those who surrounded her on their daily walks. Mom told me that in the winter months while she was there, school age children would loiter at the end of the lane and stare at them. The mothers-to-be felt vulnerable to their taunting with the absence of leaves providing privacy from the outside world. I read that it was during a 50th year class reunion that one woman admitted that, as a child, she made catcalls and offered disparaging looks from across the creek bed only to discover, as an adult, that she had been born in the Home. I wondered if the thought of her actions haunted her as much as my conflicted view of the Home haunted me. The difference is she was just a child unaware of her history, and I am an adult who is fully aware of my connection to the Home. Were her feelings of remorse for taunting unwed mothers similar to my guilt for having such conflicting views of the Home?

My three and one-half hour drive home seemed to take forever. All I could think about was opening the Evangeline Reams' book that I had been trying to acquire for several years. The book was published after her death and was given to FRH donors. To my knowledge, it was not available for sale.

I had located a copy of the book at the Columbus Metropolitan Library, but it couldn't be loaned out. It was not available to access online. I contacted the library at Malone University, but the librarian was unable to help me locate one to purchase. I called around to all the Columbus area bookstores who sold old books. No luck.

On May 2, 2019, WOSU Video Media put together an online video about Evangeline's life that was presented by a young woman from the Columbus Metropolitan Library. Her resource was the same book I had been unable to borrow from the library.

Finally, I had a copy. That night, I read the book from cover to cover, and several more times over the next few weeks. Miss Reams definitely had a well-lived life.

Equally amazing was the fact that one of the brochures Blythe Ann chose to loan to me contained information that my friend, Lynn who had been at the Home in 1969, found valuable. No coincidences.

The next two months went by too quickly. I found myself reading and re-reading everything I had been given. I took copious notes from the brochures meant for the eyes of the donors of the past, and made multiple timelines to keep track of the Homes' changes through the years.

On February 6, 2021, I fulfilled my promise to take back the literature I had borrowed. It would be a short, sweet visit for Blythe Ann and me. My husband accompanied me so he could meet the mystery woman I'd been telling him about over the past three and one-half years. We met Blythe's husband that day, too. They invited us into their home, which had originally been the caretaker's home when it was built in 1964. Their ranch style home and an apartment, built in 1960, are located behind the Home. The family moved out of the big house and into these homes in 2011.

After a long hug and introductions, the men continued chatting in the living room while Blythe Ann led me to the kitchen where she put together a box of homemade Angel Cinnamon Rolls, also known as Franzbrötchen.

When researching the origin of these delectable rolls, I learned that a baker in Hamburg-Altona is given the distinction of having invented this delicious puff pastry as a result of the occupation of Hamburg by the French army back in the days when Napoleon invaded and conquered most of Europe. They were specifically made for the French soldiers, who craved food similar to what they had in France. You can't make and bake these rolls in two hours or even a day. They are works of art and require extensive resting time and two pre-doughs. Blythe Ann told me that she and her mother would typically bake these for conferences at the Home. What a generous labor of love. Not only do they take a very long time to make, but to perfect. This time, she had help from two younger generations. They were specifically made to be given to the Home's new owner at the closing.

She had saved a box for me, and they were fabulous! The importance of the original concept and Blythe Ann's generosity were not lost on me. Coming home. Feeling at home. Being welcomed home. My sister/friend chose to gift me with all of those, and then proceeded to add a sweet treat as we hugged and said our good-byes. We have not seen each other since that day. We text one another as time permits. Another blessing bestowed upon us by our all-knowing God.

We didn't enter the Home this time. My husband would only know about it through our conversations. The new owners would take possession within weeks, and it felt intrusive to inquire about going in or even walking around it. However, my last image of the Home was lovely. There was snow on the ground, and I couldn't help but think of Mom and wonder how much snow she trudged through while carrying me. It reminded me of her Christmas village, which was meticulously set up in her kitchen each year. She always added lots of glittery snow on top of the artificial snow made specifically for villages. The Home's snow just barely covered the grass, but a bright blue sky and lovely sunlight dappling through the tree branches caused the snow to sparkle, just like the glitter. Tears welled up in my eyes as we slowly passed the Home and drove down the lane for the last time. It was perfect. Just perfect.

The side trip to the Home was not what I expected, but from the moment it began, I felt comfortable taking it. Blythe Ann referred to it as being welcomed home, and I was delighted with her sentiment. However, my mother described it as an unwelcoming place of judgment. The polar opposite perceptions became a deep chasm with no obvious bridge connecting them.

From the onset, I was curious and don't recall sensing conflict regarding my initial assessment of the Home. In 2017, I knew nothing about its history. I was simply excited to see what my birthplace looked like. It had been years since my birth mother had lived there, and its function and the people who provided it had changed. Initially, I allowed myself to only focus on the stately Home, and how it had evolved in its purpose over the years.

I permitted limited acknowledgement of that feeling in my journal entries. Blythe Ann was so enthusiastic about the Home's ministries in the Hitch era, and it wasn't until months after my second visit that I began to dig deeper into the Home's unwed mother days. I needed to resolve my perception of the Home with that of my birth mother and my new acquaintance.

Until recently, I was unaware of how I was trying to tip the scales in favor of the Home's amazing longevity of relevance for those in need. One of my journal entries describes my deep desire for Mom to have known the Home's unique ministries and their positive impact over the years. I was inclined to pass off Mom's impression of the Home, and those within it, as a result of her feisty nature. If she had been able to see the full picture, perhaps she wouldn't have been so negative about her experience. This line of thinking may have been what motivated me while learning more about the Home's original purpose. I wrote about finding captivating information about the Home, and how good it felt to know more about it.

Mom thought the Quaker's conservative attitude was sometimes cruel and borderline mean, which left her thinking they saw her as flawed and unworthy. Perhaps my mother's state of mind and negative attitude toward their rigid rules had caused her to be unpleasant to them. Maybe the same was true of my new acquaintance, Lynn. I read about young women who walked away from this very Home, in the 1950s, believing it was a good experience, considering the circumstances. There were those who felt welcomed and accepted, experienced a safe delivery, and obtained practical skills to take back home with them. Some had developed a personal relationship with Jesus and were eager to begin again. I wanted to neatly wrap up these dual impressions in a box labeled "misunderstood."

Very recently, I had the privilege of seeing the Home through the eyes of a nurse who had worked at the Friends Rescue Home briefly, in the late 1960s. She admitted she had been as young as some of the women in her care, and that she was a recently graduated nurse with no experience with pregnancy beyond that of her nursing classes. Fortunately for her, there was a more experienced nurse on staff working alongside her. Her insights regarding the staff's strengths and weaknesses enlightened me. She told me a number of the staff members were childless, and had no reference point from which to understand the unwed mother's emotional or physical state. I hadn't considered the possibility that the staff were inexperienced, or ill-equipped to deal with the unwed mother's changes throughout her pregnancy, and therefore found it challenging to understand the young woman's situation. Perhaps some staff members believed that the unwed mothers should be browbeaten into submission, and relied on that tactic rather than demonstrating compassion. She was quick to add her belief that most staff members genuinely cared about the young woman who walked through the door. Her reflections caused me to realize that I wasn't allowing human nature, societal mores, and inexperience to filter some of the staff's responses to the young women in their care. I had convinced myself it was all about then and now thinking, from society's viewpoint, instead of the fact that some staff members were not equipped or able to handle the job they were assigned to fulfill.

Months later, it became clear to me that no amount of wonderful godly acts accomplished within the walls of that dwelling would absolve the insurmountable emotional pain experienced by some of the young women.

When I walked through the Home the final time, I was reminded of conversations with my birth mother and her experience in the 50s, and I felt a deep sense of sadness for Mom and my friend, who was there in 1969. I was disappointed and angry that some of the staff had made them feel so miserable while they were there. I had assumed the staff treated the girls with kindness and respect, just like the author of their faith.

For years, I focused on the impressive goal of the ministry instead of the reality of what it was like for my mom and friend. It took my friend and the nurse to help me take off my rose-colored glasses, and dig deeper until the truth was all I could clearly see, filter eliminated. God's timing. Only grace for those who unknowingly caused pain for the unwed mothers resolved my inner conflict. I believe the majority of staff members did show compassion over the years. I've read many stories from unwed mothers who found this Home to be exactly what it was intended to be; a safe haven for them. More times than not, I want to believe the unwed mother was served with kindness.

A strong sense of gratitude for my first home remains. I am convinced God sent Evangeline and then, me, there for a reason. However, I will intentionally separate the providential home from the imperfect people who occupied its space. I will tip the scales in favor of those who lifted up generations of people by providing assistance to those in need throughout the years of the Home's existence. The amazing story of this Home's purposeful existence remains incredible to this day. In 2022, the Home had been in existence for 117 years. God willing, life changing ministries will continue within those hallowed walls for decades to come.

Jan Schiffer. (2021). Christian Conference Center. [Photograph]. Columbus, Ohio.

—Chapter 19—
Finding The Rest Of Me: Investigating My First Home

My biological mom never knew about Evangeline Reams. No one, in either of my families, would have had any association with her, or heard about her. And yet, her life's journey touched thousands of lives, female and male. Miss Reams chose a life of service and in so doing, positively impacted generations of women's lives in Ohio, including mine. My story would be incomplete without sharing part of Evangeline's incredible journey and her influence on my life fifty years before my birth.

Until I stumbled onto a brief online account of her life in May of 2019, I had not heard of Evangeline Reams or her incredible impact in Columbus, Ohio, since 1900. Before her parents were married, her father, who was of Quaker parentage, ran away and enlisted in the army during the Civil War, without his parents' consent. The Quakers are pacifists, a group who believe violence and war are unjustifiable. To make matters worse in the eyes of the Friends Church, he came home and married a woman of Methodist faith. A year before Evangeline's birth, her father was brought before the Friends with two complaints lodged against him. He had gone to war and had not married a

Quaker. He didn't apologize and was excommunicated.

Evangeline was born near Zanesfield, Ohio, on September 25, 1868. Perhaps because they were no longer welcome in the Friends Church, her parents felt the need to make a covenant with God that if her mother's life was spared, they would dedicate their daughter to the Lord. There was nothing to indicate either one of them were in danger during the pregnancy, according to Evangeline's autobiography.

Evangeline asked Jesus into her heart before she was nine years old, and before her father was permitted back into the Friends Church. Shortly afterward, he attended a revival, and at that gathering went forward and invited Jesus into his life.

As a child, Evangeline was unusually shy and not in good health. Due to her delicate condition, her doctor told her parents she would not enjoy a very long life. She didn't begin school until she was eight and missed many days due to illnesses. It was during this time, while she was praying, that she got her first call to be a missionary – nudge. She heard the voice again, at the age of sixteen, but she ignored the call because her mother didn't want her to become a missionary. After a year of ignoring the nudge and feeling heavy hearted, she became an active part of the church and prayed for God to show her His plan.

As a young woman, she was offered marriage but she chose to refuse after seeking God's approval and not receiving it. One night while on her knees in prayer, she recalled the Lord revealing a vision of the work He had created for her to do. She was to be a chosen "vessel" to provide support to others! "She had a vision of the slums, the brothels, the saloons and of young women who were being lured to death and destruction in them."

Two years would pass before a traveling minister would enlighten her about the meaning of the word *slums*, as she had never been exposed to that kind of life. She was led to new places near her home, where she was able to help others find safety. After telling her what life in the slums looked like, she knew this was her mission. He made arrangements for her to go to Columbus, and it was during that quick trip to the slums, where she had opportunities to share her unique ability to help others in these circumstances, that her vision was made real to her. She couldn't wait to tell her family and friends back home, but they still didn't approve. After a few months of prayer, however, her parents consented, and she returned to Columbus, Ohio, on October 12, 1900.

At the age of 32, with no money and no connections, Evangeline began her work in Columbus at a place called "Mission Hall" on Canal St., where she continued to serve for over three years. For a short period of time after this, she worked in a section of Columbus, known as Fly Town, before returning home for three months to rest. Soon after that, the Friends of Highland Avenue Church sent for her to begin working with them in their mission on West Broad St., back in Columbus. It was during this time that she started visiting saloons/bars and brothels and began her search for a shelter for the unfortunate girls she was meeting who were caught up in prostitution and drugs, and with little to no hope.

It was remarkable that she felt comfortable entering such places having never been exposed to them before leaving home. People would remark about her easy and natural approach. She said her confidence came from the Lord's leading, not hers. The first shelter she secured was in the home of the pastor of the Highland Avenue Friends Church, named Fred Cope. The first girl was cared for by Etta Cope, his wife. It wasn't long before Fred became the first president of the Friends Rescue Home in 1905. One account of her growing passion for a shelter for women reads as follows:

"One day she was called to visit a girl who was dying in an attic on Front Street. The girl would not tell her right name or the place in which she lived before coming into her life of sin. A sad picture, the rats running over her bed and eating the meals that were brought to her. She would not accept Christ. Coming down the stairs, eight girls said they would go with her, but where could she take them? No home was open for the girls. Weeping with them she said, "Good-bye," with her heart breaking. As she came out on the street, she was still weeping and praying that God would answer her prayer for a shelter for them. He did! A lady gave her five dollars to start a home. In prayer that day, she and the congregation asked the Lord to double it as many times as He saw fit. He answered. A man was touched by God to give $200 for a home."

Perhaps a reading of this account led in the decision of The Highland Ave. Friends Church to help, especially after Evangeline voiced her concern to them for the rescue of fallen girls. The next step was taken, and a home on N. Harris Ave. was rented in April of 1905, and was purchased the following year. The Friends Church helped maternity cases, and also took a number of cases from the courts and slums. The Home was incorporated and endorsed by the State Board of Charities. It was there that she was said to have had a vision of the Home on North Powell. She believed God's promise to provide and told her friends that someday they would move into the country. She prayed about it for five years.

In 1911, Evangeline worked to establish a certified birthing center in the Harris Avenue Home so that women would not have to leave the Home to have their babies in a hospital and then return. As a licensed maternity hospital, it was incorporated under the laws of Ohio from the Board of State Charities and the State Board of Health.

From the beginning, she was interested in the whole person – mentally, physically and spiritually. She created an atmosphere in which one could get an education, be trained for a job outside the home and provided with childcare service after the birth, if the woman wished to raise the child. This was remarkable in the early 1900s. It was said that she raised the $1,000 for the monthly needs of the home all by herself.

Thanks, in part, to the sale of Harris Ave. as well as a multitude of letters of endorsement from community leaders in the legal and medical fields in 1915, funds were secured to purchase two properties (278 and 282) on E. 13th Ave., in 1916.

Below are examples of the many letters written to the Friends regarding Evangeline's significant contribution to the community and encouragement for her to continue the valuable ministry.

> UNITED STATES
> DEPARTMENT OF JUSTICE.
> LOCAL WHITE SLAVE OFFICER.
>
> COLUMBUS, O., March 19, 1915.
>
> *To Whom it May Concern:*
>
> I have had ample occasion to observe the work of the Friends Rescue Home and I think it meets a great need in Columbus, and that the citizens ought to contribute enough to at least quadruple the present size and equipment.
>
> I have been able to find no other home in Columbus which will take and shelter women who are really down and out, women who have gone any distance into the gutter. Miss Evangeline Reams, Field Secretary, who is in charge, has unusual ability for this work, and also the patience and optimism which are so desirable. No work is more needed in Columbus.
>
> Respectfully,
>
> ROBERT E. PFEIFFER,
> *U. S. Local White Slave Officer.*

> SHERIFF'S OFFICE, FRANKLIN COUNTY, COLUMBUS, OHIO.
> CHARLES L. RESCH, *Sheriff.*
>
> COLUMBUS, O., March 19, 1915.
>
> EVANGELINE REAMS, *Field Secretary, Friends Rescue Home,*
> *Columbus, Ohio.*
>
> I take great pleasure in commending the fine work accomplished in your Rescue Home, thru the earnest efforts of Evangeline Reams, Field Secretary, and her corps of assistants.
>
> The number of young girls that have been helped, after serving a sentence in the County jail, has been many, and the fruits of this work can be only too plainly seen, through work of rescuing the fallen from the life of sin and lifted to one of unspeakable joy and happiness.
>
> I sincerely hope that your work will be more fully realized by the general public and that your present quarters may be enlarged so you will be able to take care of these unfortunate girls for which you are compelled to turn away for want of more room, which to you, I am aware is heart rendering indeed.
>
> I want to thank you from the bottom of my heart for the good work you have accomplished with the girls turned over to you by me out of the County jail. It is alone God's work, and it is my wish that for your success you may continue to save these poor unfortunate girls.
>
> We are, very sincerely,
>
> C. L. RESCH,
> *Sheriff of Franklin Co., O.*
> W. M. SLACK,
> *Jailer of Franklin Co., O.*

Evangeline Reams: A Sketch of Her Life and the Story of the Founding of the Friends Rescue Home (43, 44), Clark, H. H. (n.d.) (Permission granted by the Archives Committee of Malone University and representatives from EFC-ER.)

Friends Rescue Home (1925)

Friends Rescue Home (1925) Second Homes. p.16

Within two short years, these houses became too small for the number of beds that were needed. In the book about her life, I read that one night, a girl entered the home, but there were no available beds. Evangeline gave up her bed, and instead of sleeping she remained awake all-night praying about the burden she was feeling.

The following morning in the dining room where they were assembled, seventeen of the twenty-two girls asked Jesus into their hearts and were saved. Her heart was no longer burdened. She knew what she was called to do, and she pursued it with passion. After her usual busy morning of running errands, she went into a real estate office where, hanging on the wall, she saw a picture of the N. Hague property, as it was known before it became 245 N. Powell Ave.

She said God had spoken to her heart and said, "This is the Friends Rescue Home." She inquired about the information regarding the property and told them about her first vision regarding the future home of the society being in the country. After relaying the vision at the office, she told the realtor, "You will never sell it, for it is to be the Friends Rescue Home." He must have thought she was a woman of integrity because she was given the keys to the house and drove out to look it over.

She said, "As I walked onto the grounds, looked at the beautiful mansion, the location, the entire surroundings, I said, 'O Lord! it is too good to be true, but I will not doubt.' I stepped inside of the house, and another promise was given to me, 'Every foot of ground on which you put your feet, is yours.' In five minutes, after I looked over the house, I had appropriated every room for our different purposes. I walked out and thanked God over and over." The real estate company was unable to sell the property. During the same time period, a man offered $10,000 for the two properties on 13th Ave. Due to that man's generosity, the Rescue Home Board realized that the vision must be true. In May, 1918, a down payment of $10,000 was made, leaving a balance of $16,500. They opened the doors of the Home in the Spring of 1919.

Soon after, the story is told of a beautiful woman who drove a large car up to the Home. She told Evangeline that her doctor had sent her there because she was having heart trouble. Evangeline believed the

Lord revealed to her that this woman needed Jesus in her heart. After a conversation, the beautiful woman gave her life to the Lord and asked Evangeline what she should do next.

Evangeline replied that she should pray, read her Bible, trust in the Lord, and tell her friends about Jesus. She continued by telling her to abstain from playing cards, dancing, or any of the other "worldly" forms of entertainment. The Friends believed that by participating in these things a person might be led to more sinful acts.

The lady's friends abandoned her, and a guardian was appointed to care for her when she was no longer able to care for herself. When she passed, three years later, her will stated that the Home should receive $16,000, which paid off the balance of the mortgage at that time. There are so many similar stories about this providential Home.

Evangeline's unique ability to collect funds was paramount in keeping the Home in operation until the time of her passing at the age of 62. She was given the title, Field Secretary, which meant she was in charge of securing funds to support the ongoing work of the Home. She was invited to speak in churches of almost all denominations, and one year, in the early 1900s, she logged 10,000 miles.

This timid, sickly Quaker girl had grown to be the capable, confident woman who visited the worst possible places, and arranged the release of the girls and women as well as bringing them to a safe shelter where they were taught life skills to improve their futures. She had many remarkable experiences and talked about them with simplicity.

In the early 1900s, false "Want Ads" appeared in the local newspaper that attempted to lure innocent girls into a life of prostitution. Evangeline worked with the police in many of what we would call "sting" operations.

Evangeline began to take it upon herself to follow the ads in the local newspaper and contact the authorities if she thought there was danger to those responding. In 1915, she received letters of endorsements and appreciation from the Medical Dean of OSU, the Dept. of Public Safety (name given to the division of the police department in charge of implementing the sting operations with Evangeline), a doctor from Grant Hospital, a probate court judge, the mayor of Columbus, the Chief of Police and the U.S. Local White Slave officer, who was a deputized volunteer in charge of monitoring prostitutes after the Department of Justice eliminated the White Slave Division in 1914. At the time, the biggest concern was about soldiers getting venereal diseases from the "flappers" who were described as young girls who were promiscuous and diseased. The special agents chose middle class, respectable, white males who were usually attorneys to perform the task of monitoring.

Evangeline became the superintendent of the Gilead Social Training School for Delinquent Women at a property outside Columbus, while continuing to secure food for the current residents of the Home. Two such examples are recorded in the book about her life. She tells of the day when the Home was in need of groceries and it became very heavy on her heart to do something about it. At the time, they bought groceries and trusted that God would supply the money necessary to pay for them. "We baked our own bread, but the flour sack was empty, and no money in the treasury with which to buy more."

As she knelt down to pray about the matter, she recalled the picture of William Penn with a loaf in his hand that was used as an advertisement for one of the local bakeries in Columbus. She believed that to be a sign from God and proceeded to go to that place of business. When she entered the office, she asked to see Mr. Brennan, the owner of the bakery. He was standing in front of her and acknowledged her by name. She asked how he knew her. His response was: "I have known you these many years and know what you are doing to help others. What is on your heart?"

She told him about praying and seeing the advertisement. She said that she came to see if he would be willing to furnish the Friends Rescue Home with bread from his bakery.

His reply was "I will give you bread as long as we have a bakery." The Brennan Bread Company furnished the Friends Rescue Home with bread for eleven years, in answer to prayer, according to Evangeline.

On another occasion, a young girl in the Home asked Evangeline to pray for honey because they were almost out of their supply. Evangeline began praying, and several days later she learned of a man in Adrian, Michigan, who was straining honey for sale when the Lord spoke to him and said to send honey to the Friends Rescue Home.

"He measured out one gallon and thought that this was all he could spare. The Lord spoke to him again and said, 'Send five gallons.' He obeyed the Lord and sent it. The very day this little girl asked for the honey, God spoke to this man's heart." They were never without honey for the next ten years.

After a speaking engagement in Indiana, Evangeline died at 62 due to injuries sustained from a car hitting her as she stepped off the curb while attempting to cross the street. There was no stop sign posted at the time.

She was buried near her parents, in Goshen Quaker Cemetery, in the beautiful Marmon Valley, where she had been raised.

The book *Evangeline Reams - A Brief Sketch of Her Life and Story of The Friends Rescue Home* by author Harry H. Clark, was used to solicit funding for the Home after her death. It includes Evangeline's stories in her own words as well as events in her life as told by others.

After reading innumerable accounts of this woman's daily encounters with the downtrodden, as she called them, and all those who were in a position to help them, I am in awe of her tenacity and unwavering trust in her calling from God. Her obituary read, in part, "To review the life of Evangeline Reams is practically to tell the story of the Friends Rescue Home of Columbus, Ohio. So closely has her life's interest been associated with that work that one finds it impossible to separate them."

A mighty nudge, like a pebble tossed in calm waters has rippled far beyond what anyone but God could imagine. During her ministry, 1,700 girls, from every walk of life were brought to the Home. I'm told 4,500 babies were born while the doors of the Friends Rescue Home were open. There were over 4,000 adoptions that occurred during those years. But those precious souls are just the beginning of the ripple sent by God to Evangeline Reams. Their babies, their families, and all the generations who followed, as well as all those who were and are still touched by the ministry must be counted in this ripple effect as well. Prayers and nudges. Nudges and prayers.

—Chapter 20—
Puzzle Pieces

To my knowledge, Mom was not interested in sitting down and piecing a puzzle together. She preferred to spend her time visiting with friends and family while all were seated around her island in her kitchen. Her comfortably cushioned swivel chairs provided hours of delight as the stories, jokes and coffee flowed. She volunteered at a local soup kitchen once a week and often provided canned goods and clothing to the Samaritan House, a homeless shelter for women and their children in Lima. She loved animals and experienced a great amount of joy and satisfaction in providing treats and administering affection to each neighborhood dog or cat who wandered onto her property. Even the squirrels knew they were welcome.

When we first met, Barb had two dogs who enjoyed a carefree life with her. During the winter, she provided shelter and food for a family of feral cats close to her front door so that she could check on bedding, water and food without having to brave the winter winds. When Spring arrived, those same cats would meander through the neighborhood, soliciting scraps from anyone willing to oblige, and head to a safe, green space nearby. Occasionally, they would drop in on her just in case she had a leftover or two to offer them. Of course, she was always prepared for them, and what she provided was never a leftover. She was the neighborhood dog care-giver when their owners were on vacation or had an emergency. A large keyring containing duplicates of each of her neighbors' front door keys was always easily accessible just in case she was needed.

In the springtime, Mom enjoyed planting a variety of beautiful annual flowers in her flower beds along the sides of her house. As summer progressed, she found joy watering, weeding and proudly showing them off to those who visited. On crisp fall Saturdays and Sundays, she watched every minute of her favorite teams playing football.

Before the department stores began putting out their Christmas decorations, her Christmas village was spread across much of her kitchen counter, where she and her company could enjoy it. Each side of the kitchen sink had white felt laying close to the edges. After setting up her village, she added just the right amount of "snow" glitter. It was amazing. It was not only a delight to her grandchildren's eyes, but to all her family and friends.

She kept a daily record of the weather along with her activities in a small stenographer-type book. Her house was immaculate. Every Saturday morning was reserved for a call from Linda. On Sundays, she attended church. She read her Bible and prayed throughout the week. She didn't have time for a puzzle.

On the other hand, I love to work on a good puzzle, especially on a cold winter day. I always begin with the outside pieces to frame it. Then, I look for pieces that appear to have the same colors or textures and commence the process of piecing it all together. Every so often, I imagine my life as one of those pieces. I once read an article in which readers were encouraged to carry a puzzle piece in their pockets to represent their unique presence in the world. In other words, each of us represents a small piece of the grand puzzle that is life on this earth. Each is irreplaceable and necessary in order for the puzzle to be completed. What an excellent reminder of our value.

Sometimes, I try to imagine putting together a puzzle without the benefit of the picture on the box top that shows me how the puzzle should look when it is finished. While taking this journey to find the rest of me, I imagined this unpictured puzzle in front of me, with pieces that represent my complete life, beginning to end. Yet, I am well aware of the fact that none of us can witness our finished puzzle until our life's end; it has yet to be created. I'd like to think God knows our completed puzzle, even though He has given us a free will to choose our destiny until our final breath. We fill in the pieces according to the choices we make each day.

I've had the outside pieces of my life framed for a very long time. Knowing I was adopted was a part of that framework, but beyond knowing the beginning of my existence, there was much left to be discovered. The remainder was framed with my adoptive family, friends and significant acquaintances in my youth. Then, college, marriage, our careers, and our children completed the frame.

I might never have met my biological family, and learned so much about myself and them had it not been for my cousin Winni's slip of tongue. Thanks to her and God's nudge, I began this expedition into my past, and continued to unearth more missing pieces. Each fragment has positively impacted the landscape of my puzzle, my life.

Several years ago, I called Winni to thank her for telling me I was adopted. We shared our feelings about what transpired on that warm summer day when we were youngsters, and I disclosed how the trajectory of my life changed because of the secret being revealed. Briefly, I described meeting my biological family and the seventeen years of knowing Barb. A few years later, Winni met my sister, Linda, who was vacationing in Florida. I had told Linda where my cousin was working and that's where they met. It was the first time my adoptive and biological worlds "collided" openly.

When our daughter got married, in 2011, she wanted to invite her Aunt Linda and her Uncle Walt. I informed her that I was in complete agreement, but there wouldn't be an introduction on that occasion, unless they were the ones to initiate it. In my opinion, it wasn't the time or place. Both families attended the wedding and an informal introduction was never instigated. After the wedding, I found out neither of them figured out who the other was, which surprised me because it wasn't a particularly large wedding. They never met.

A few years ago, Winni and her husband came to our home for a visit. It was the first time we had seen each other since our telephone conversation. We live 2,444 miles away from each other. It is reassuring to have that sweet peace in knowing it is well between us.

In my mind's eye, I reflect upon the parts of my puzzle that are complete and I find it incredible; full of interesting side trips, unexpected surprises, and a pleasant, peaceful balance. As I fill in the middle, the portion where both worlds have so beautifully come together, I am astounded by the way in which God has led my heart, as well as my hands and feet, in each direction. The nudges! I see His handiwork, just as one sees it in an intricate puzzle created by the best of craftspeople. As the Bible verse says, "And the LORD, He is the One who goes before you. He will be with you. He will not leave you nor forsake you; do not fear nor be dismayed."

He is the master builder of my puzzle and I am in awe of what He has done throughout my life's journey.

Contacting the Health Dept and receiving my birth certificate through the mail, in record time, was surprising. Connecting the dots, by locating documents at the local library and the county courthouse in days rather than weeks, was phenomenal. Discovering a website with information that quickly led me to the place of my birth, was truly remarkable. Becoming friends with the Home's owner and all the other interesting and thoughtful people God chose to place in my path have been pure blessings. Developing a relationship with a woman who experienced the Home, years after my mother was there, has been extraordinary. In my opinion, it has all been God ahead of me, prompting me, and staying beside me. His timing remains perfect. Connecting my past to my present provided me with a deeper understanding of myself. My hope is that I will continue to have the courage to move when the nudge prompts me, to step out on the ledge of faith, which has caused me to walk into my purpose.

My first glimpse of my mom was from her front door window. That day she had no idea how her life would change…again. Her early years had been filled with turmoil, some of her own making. When we met, she was middle-aged and settled into a quiet life with her revered family, faithful friends and beloved animals. The constants were a strong will and an acceptance of the life she had chosen. For her short stature, she packed a punch in her resolve to move on with laughter and a fierce love for those in her circle. And so it was that she walked with me through the next seventeen years of our lives.

Even though Mom didn't appear to care for puzzles, I have felt her presence since the beginning of this search to find the rest of me. My sister once told me she found Mom alone in their living room, listening to a record by country singer, Jim Reeves. As I composed the parts of Mom's story, I listened to one of his vinyls I had purchased a few years ago. Songs like "It Hurts So Much to See You Go," "Just Out of Reach," "After Loving You," and "I Won't Forget You," sung in his velvety smooth voice allowed my imagination to freely flow back to what might have been her feelings all those many years ago. Frequently, the song's lyrics brought me to tears as I attempted to understand how difficult it must have been to be a birth mother with no child and no husband. The melancholy I imagined Barb experiencing in those moments washed over me and I mourned her losses. Some days I couldn't write a word. It hurt too much to consider her hidden pain…. unbearable and heartbreaking.

Yet, far more often, I sensed her laughter when I mused over a very colorful piece of her history as it was gently placed within my puzzle. I felt the warmth of her smile just over my shoulder when I discovered an article or a person with a significant bit of information. It has been my story, but she has been woven into each and every moment of it as my biological mother. Since the beginning of my journey, many of the voices who provided meaningful answers to my constant barrage of questions are now silenced. As each has passed, I'm reminded of their willingness to trust me with their truth, even when it wasn't pleasant. Each nudge to contact them has provided me with a fuller picture of how we fit together at some point in this life and I am grateful for each of them.

Occasionally, I receive timely tips, valuable information and insights regarding the past and how it connects to me. It's exciting to know there is more out there to be discovered and I continue to sense my mother's presence and energy within me. As each unique and colorful puzzle piece is placed in its proper location, it draws me closer to the culmination of the puzzle and to the completion of us. I have been, and continue to be, blessed beyond measure. Thank you, Mom!

References

Brandon, A. R., Pitts, S., Denton, W. H., Stringer, C. A., & Evans, H. M. (2009). A History of the theory of prenatal attachment. *Journal of Prenatal & Perinatal Psychology & Health*, 23(4), 201–222.

Clark, H. H. (1991) *Evangeline Reams: A Brief Sketch of Her Life and the Story of the Founding of the Friends Rescue Home*. Damascus, Ohio. Friends Rescue Home, Board of the Ohio Yearly Meeting.

Columbus Neighborhoods. (2019). *Evangeline Reams – Notable Women*. [Video]. WOSU-PBS. https://video.wosu.org/video/evangeline-reams-tmt8c6/

Darznik, J. (2022). *Blame it on Jazz*. [Article]. Hollywood Progressive. https://hollywoodprogressive.com/music/blame-it-on-jazz

Donahue, P. (1992). *First Time National Exposure for Mothers of Adoption Loss: CUB founder, Lee Campbell, Speaks Out*. [Television rebroadcast]. NBC.

Friends Rescue Home. (1915). Report of the Friends Rescue Home, Columbus, Ohio, From 1905-1915. [Pamphlet]. E. J. Heer Printing, Co., 1915. Columbus, Ohio., 26. http://digital-collections.columbuslibrary.org/digital/collection/memory/id/73535/

Friends Rescue Home. (1950's). FRIENDS HOME – A Home for Unwed Mothers [Trifold Brochure]. Friends Rescue Home, Board of Ohio Yearly Meeting.

Inside Facts on the Social Evil. (1914, June 25). *Marysville Journal Tribune*, p. 2.

New King James Version Bible. (1983). Thomas Nelson, Inc.

"Obituary: John Holley Roys," *Democrat and Chronicle,* Rochester, New York, (1940, January 10), page 30. https://newspaper.com/article/democrat-and-chronicle-obituary-for-john//122076094

Ohio History Connection. (n.d.). Ohio Reformatory for Women. https://ohiohistory.libguides.com/prison/OhioReformatoryforWomen

Ohio Yearly Meeting of Friends. (1933). The third-floor dormitory, labor and delivery room. [Photographs]. Friends Rescue Home

Pliley, J. R. (2014). *Policing Sexuality – The Mann Act and The Making of the FBI*. Harvard University Press.

Rosenberg, G. (2016, November 23). Curious Cbus: *What Happened to Columbus's Streetcars?* https://news.wosu.org/news/2016-11-23/curious-cbus-what-happened-to-columbus- streetcars

Schiffer, J. (1990, April 27). Give your child a chance; consider the adoption option. *The Lima News*

Singing the Song in My Heart. (2015, July 22). Song Story: *Barbara Ann by the Beach Boys*. https://singingthesonginmyheart.com/barbara-ann-by-the-beach-boys

Social Welfare History Project. (2014). *Florence Crittenton Homes: A History*. https://socialwelfare.library.vcu.edu/programs/child-welfarechild-labor/florence-crittenton-homes-history/

Thomas, R. (1955, May 8). Haven for unwed mothers: 50th Anniversary marked by Friends Rescue Home. *Columbus Dispatch*, p. 26E.

Wilson-Buterbaugh, K. (2007). The Baby Scoop Era Research Initiative. *Research and Inquiry into Adoption Practice.*, 1945-1972, p. 1. https://babyscoopera.com/home/what-was-the-baby-scoop-era/

Unverzagt, K. (1960's). The Friends Rescue Home [Photograph]. http://facebook.com/HistoricalWestSideColumbusOhio/photos/a.385153311543116/520930027965443/

Acknowledgments

Without the expertise, encouragement, and patience of the wonderful people listed below, this book wouldn't be in your hands. My deep gratitude to:

Blythe Ann Cooper, my sister/friend, who wholeheartedly shared her home's rich history and her warm heart with me. Truly, she became my bonus family.

Ed Walsh, Director of Church Health and Finance & Administration, and the Archives Committee at Malone University, for generously allowing me permission to tell a snippet of Evangeline Reams' amazing life story and the story of the Friends Rescue Home.

Lynda C. Porter, my extremely talented illustrator, for her intuitive gift of translating my gibberish into the spectacular cover I envisioned. I appreciated her willingness to collaborate with me, her cheerful, uplifting comments, and the friendship we have developed in the process.

Lynn Lauber, my gifted manuscript editor, and beloved confidant, for working with me through my first and second rough drafts with professionalism and compassion, and willingly staying connected throughout this book's evolution. Our stories are forever intertwined.

*Lynda and Lynn are both Lima Senior High School graduates, like the author.

Mary Popham, my inspiring copy editor, for coming alongside me and this project at just the right time. She saved me from the pitfalls present in a debut manuscript with her excellent editing and just the right amount of encouragement.

Erin (O'Neil) Lovelien, owner of Fishtail Publishing, for sticking with me on this roller coaster ride until I was ready for her to work her magic. I appreciate her commitment to excellence as a publisher.

My family and friends, who motivated me to press forward during the seven-year process of writing and editing. Whether you provided me a quiet place to stay while I pulled my thoughts and papers together without distractions, called to offer an uplifting word of encouragement when I needed it most, or listened to my rambling on about each new discovery along my journey during a casual conversation; each of you added to the completion of this book. You know who you are, and I'm indebted to you.

My sister, Linda, for being the safe keeper of our family's memories before I joined the family, and my loyal supporter.

Finally, to my dear husband, George, for being my faithful watchman and quiet advocate during my years of writing. Thank you for giving me space to pursue my dream.